Cake Mix Magic₂

125 More Easy Desserts…
Good as Homemade

JILL SNIDER

Robert
ROSE

For complete cataloguing information, see page 186.

Disclaimer
The recipes in this book have been carefully tested by our kitchen and our tasters. To the best of our knowledge, they are safe and nutritious for ordinary use and users. For those people with food or other allergies, or who have special food requirements or health issues, please read the suggested contents of each recipe carefully and determine whether or not they may create a problem for you. All recipes are used at the risk of the consumer.

We cannot be responsible for any hazards, loss or damage that may occur as a result of any recipe use.

For those with special needs, allergies, requirements or health problems, in the event of any doubt, please contact your medical adviser prior to the use of any recipe.

Design & Production: PageWave Graphics Inc.
Editor: Judith Finlayson
Copy Editor: Deborah Aldcorn
Recipe Editor: Jennifer MacKenzie
Photography: Mark T. Shapiro
Food Stylists: Kate Bush, Jill Snider
Props Stylist: Charlene Erricson
Color Scans: Colour Technologies

The publisher and author wish to express their appreciation to the following supplier of props used in the food photography:

DISHES, LINENS AND ACCESSORIES

The Crockery Barn Ltd.
1424 Yonge St.
Toronto, Ontario, M4T 1Y5
Tel: (416) 968-0976

French Country Inc.
6 Roxborough St. West
Toronto, Ontario M5R 1T8
Tel: (416) 944-2204

FLATWARE

Gourmet Settings Inc.
245 West Beaver Creek Rd., Unit 10
Richmond Hill, Ontario, L4B 1L1
Tel: 1-800-551-2649
www.gourmetsettings.com

Cover image: Apple Pinwheel Cake (page 88)

We acknowledge the financial support of the Government of Canada through the Book Publishing Industry Development Program (BPIDP) for our publishing activities.

Published by: Robert Rose Inc.
120 Eglinton Ave. E., Suite 1000, Toronto, Ontario, Canada M4P 1E2
Tel: (416) 322-6552 Fax: (416) 322-6936

Printed in Canada
2 3 4 5 6 7 8 9 10   CPL   09 08 07 06 05 04

Contents

Acknowledgments

I'd like to thank the many people involved in making the idea of a second *Cake Mix Magic* a reality. The overwhelming response to the first book was a clear indication that it filled a need in people's hectic lives and it provided the encouragement to do another.

First, my publisher, Bob Dees, who started the ball rolling in response to his customers' comments. On this book, his high degree of professionalism, combined with extreme patience, understanding, encouragement and guidance, surpassed the first, which I would have thought was impossible.

Brenda Venedam, who again typed and retyped all the copy with such painstaking accuracy that she made my proof reading job easy. Her family also tasted and commented honestly on many of the recipes, providing an invaluable combination of opinion from both kids and adults. I knew the dishes that disappeared overnight were winners.

My mother, who put up with my ridiculous working hours and never complained about having an omelet for dinner, again. My sister and nieces, who served the recipes at every possible occasion and made a point of telling everyone their source.

The talented, creative team who makes all the cakes, cookies, bars, squares and desserts look amazing, yet realistic and achievable. Mark Shapiro, the photographer; Kate Bush, the food stylist; Charlene Erricson, the prop stylist; Andrew Smith, Joseph Gisini, Kevin Cockburn and Daniella Zanchetta of PageWave Graphics, who diligently worked through editorial, design, layouts and production to put it all together.

Although I was skeptical about being able to do another book of recipes that would please me as much as the first had done, I now must admit that practice truly does make perfect. In this book, there are a lot of favorites I couldn't eliminate if I had to. I hope from the wide variety of recipes included that you, too, will find many favorites of your own.

Introduction

Cake in some form plays an important role in the ritual of our lives — whether it is a coffee cake in the morning, a teatime treat, a lunchbox sweet, a late-night dessert or a snack at any time during the day. And, of course, a birthday party without cake just wouldn't be a proper celebration. Part of its charm is that cake can be as plain and simple or as elegant and decadent as the occasion demands and this versatility has helped to make it an indispensable part of daily life.

In today's hectic world, there are fewer and fewer hours of free time available to bake. Consequently, people who enjoy baking have an even greater need for shortcuts that don't sacrifice quality. Anyone who bakes from scratch knows two things: baking cakes can be time-consuming and it can produce disappointing results. Although I love to bake from scratch, I'm happy to use any convenience food that saves time and still meets my high standards for quality. I call it speedy scratch baking! That's why I always like to have a cake mix — or two — and a few other ingredients on hand. It rules out the excuse that you don't have time to bake and is a great way to be prepared for the unexpected.

A Duncan Hines cake mix is the perfect shortcut solution, because beginning with the best always gets you off to a great start. Since the ingredients are already measured accurately and are consistently reliable, a mix saves preparation steps, such as measuring, sifting and creaming. Using a cake mix also greatly reduces the number of ingredients required to create a dazzling dessert. You can still add rich and flavorful ingredients such as eggs, sour cream, butter, nuts, chocolate and fruit, which give cake that distinctive "homemade" taste that no bakery cake can match.

Another benefit of cake mixes is their tolerance. Mixes are formulated to withstand minor variables such as overmixing, undermixing, oven temperature variations, measuring utensil discrepancies, different mixers and pans and a variety of added ingredients. The risk of a disaster is greatly reduced. In fact, it is almost a guarantee that you will be proud of your masterpiece. But if, by chance, something goes wrong, don't apologize. My foolproof solution is to serve it warm with a big scoop of vanilla ice cream. Everyone will be happy and none the wiser!

In *Cake Mix Magic 2,* I've included a selection of cakes that will carry you through every occasion. The recipes are easy to follow and use ingredients you likely have on hand or can easily find at your local grocery store. Each chapter offers a wide variety of flavors and I've made suggestions for variations on the cakes and frostings to suit different tastes. I'm sure you'll think of more combinations as well. With a little imagination and creativity, the possibilities are endless.

Single-Layer Cakes are usually quick and easy to prepare. They are often glazed or frosted right in the pan — an ideal choice for casual entertaining, bake sales, potlucks and lunchboxes since they are easy to carry and serve.

Multi-Layer Cakes take more time to complete as the layers are filled, frosted and decorated. However, the cake portion is often very simple to make and, frequently, it can be prepared in advance. The cakes in this section range from simple and easy to fairly elaborate. When you pull out all the stops, the results can be spectacular and they are usually well worth the extra time and effort. These lovely creations are just the ticket for those special occasions when you want to dazzle your guests.

Tube & Bundt Cakes can suit both everyday and special occasions. Generally quick and easy to make, they lend themselves to the addition of other ingredients such as nuts, pureed vegetables and fruits. If for no other reason, they are impressive because of their shape. Often a burst of flavor is added by brushing syrup on the warm cake and letting it soak in. These cakes may be served plain or finished with a simple glaze, a dusting of confectioner's sugar or a basic frosting.

Coffee Cakes are perennial favorites. As the name implies, they make a perfect match for a cup of steaming coffee, cappuccino or tea, anytime of the day. These cakes tend to be less sweet than most and they often contain fresh fruit.They are always wonderful served warm. One taste of the Raspberry Streusel Cake, a personal favorite, will sell you on their special charms.

Quick Breads & Muffins are another favorite accompaniment for coffee. As the name implies, they don't require a lot of preparation time and offer many of the same satisfactions as freshly baked yeast breads.

Angel Food Cakes have a unique texture: they are extremely moist and light as a feather. And the cakes can be enhanced with other ingredients such as fresh fruit, for a refreshingly light dessert such as Raspberry Angel Trifle, or with cream and chocolate, for a heavenly but decadent concoction such as Tiramisu.

Varieties of **cheesecake** are another treat which are easier to make using a mix as a base. The constant favorites are always a perfect choice to serve to guests.

Special Occasion Cakes require a little more time, but they, too, are worth the effort. Have some fun during holidays with family projects such as the Gingerbread Carousel and the Frosty the Snowman Cake.

Cookies, Bars & Squares will really convince you that cake mixes are versatile. These cookie recipes taste better than most cookie mixes and the bars taste as though they were made from scratch. Use the recipes from these sections to easily prepare lunchbox treats, Christmas cookies or other special delights.

I've included a chapter called **Desserts:** it offers recipes that start with a cake mix but they aren't really cakes. Comfort food cobblers, crumbles and crisps are made easy. You'll also find chilled desserts such as mousse cakes and many make-ahead dishes here.

This book wouldn't be complete without **Frostings, Fillings & Glazes** to finish your masterpieces. There's more than one to suit every cake. Mix, match, choose your favorites and enjoy!

Among the many recipes, I'm sure you'll find a few that will become your favorites. I've tried to include something for every taste and occasion. Use the recipes as a starting point and add your own touches. Most of all — *enjoy cake baking — the easy and delicious way!*

Baking Equipment

PANS

Today's baking pans are not as standardized as they once were. They differ in size and shape from older ones and they vary from one manufacturer to another. The labeling consists of a mix of imperial and metric measurements, which is often confusing. I recommend using the pan size specified in the recipes, as using a size that is not called for can affect results. However, since cake mixes are more tolerant of variations than cakes baked from scratch, you have more latitude in terms of the pans you use. Feel free to substitute a pan that is similar in dimension and volume, but don't use pans smaller in volume, as the cake may overflow. It is usually safe to use a pan that is slightly larger than the one specified, although the cake will be shallower and require less baking time. You can interchange shapes (e.g., round instead of square) if the volume is the same and the pan is not much deeper, shallower, longer or shorter. To measure a pan, take the measurements on the inside, across the top. To confirm the volume of a pan, fill it with water and pour the liquid into a measuring cup.

You will need these common pans to prepare the cakes in this book:

- A 13- by 9-inch (3 L) pan
- Three 8-inch (20 cm) round pans
- Three 9-inch (23 cm) round pans
- A 10-inch (3 L) Bundt pan
- A 10-inch (4 L) tube pan
- An 8- to 10-inch (20 to 25 cm) springform pan
- Two 8½- by 4½- inch (1.5 L) or 9- by 5-inch (2 L) loaf pans
- Two muffin (cupcake) pans (12 cups each)
- A 17- by 11-inch (3 L) jellyroll pan
- Baking sheets, without sides
- A 13- by 9-inch (3 L) glass baking pan

I prefer good quality, shiny metal pans for baking. They bake evenly and don't rust. If you use glass pans, decrease the oven temperature by 25°F (10°C). If using nonstick pans, follow the manufacturer's directions. Most recommend reducing the temperature by 25°F (10°C) since nonstick surfaces, especially dark ones, bake faster. This adjustment is especially important for large cakes because the edges will overbake before the center is done.

MIXER

Use an electric countertop mixer or a good-quality hand mixer, not the heavy-duty commercial type, which are too powerful for normal home use. If you do a lot of baking, the countertop model is much more efficient and easier to use than a hand mixer.

BOWLS

Every kitchen needs a variety of bowls in different sizes for mixing ingredients. Have a few of each size — small, medium and large. I prefer metal or glass. Plastic does not work well for beaten egg whites. Most of the batters in this book are prepared in a large mixer bowl. I refer to the bowl needed for electric mixer as a mixer bowl. If this isn't specified, other bowls will do (for example, when mixing a crumble topping, or fruit with sugar).

RACKS

Wire racks are essential for cooling cakes. Choose stainless steel, since they won't rust and have a long life. It's a good idea to have a variety of sizes (round, square, rectangle) to suit the size of cakes you are making. Look for racks that have narrow spaces between the wires. This is important so small items such as muffins and cookies don't slip through. To avoid having rack marks on the top of your cake, keep one rack covered with a thick tea towel pinned securely in place. When necessary, remove the towel for washing.

KNIVES

A long, sharp serrated knife with a blade about 12 inches (30 cm) long makes cutting cakes horizontally a breeze. Some people prefer to use dental floss for an even slice. Try both methods and pick your favorite. Electric knives are excellent for angel food cake. A good quality chef's knife is essential for chopping ingredients.

MICROWAVE-SAFE BOWL OR DISH

These are ideal for melting chocolate, heating liquids and dissolving gelatin mixtures and so on. Usually, one each in small and medium sizes works well.

SAUCEPANS

Two heavy saucepans, one small and one medium-size, are necessary to prepare the finishing parts of some cakes, such as caramelized sugar and cooked puddings.

KITCHEN SHEARS

A sharp pair of kitchen scissors is a handy accessory. This tool makes easy work of cutting dried fruits such as apricots.

PASTRY BAG AND TIPS

These are useful for finishing cakes and not difficult to use. All you need to make attractive decorations is a few basic tips. I prefer the disposable bags for convenience. Choose a large and small star tip and a small round tip for writing. For simple decorations such as writing names and drawing outlines, a plastic squeeze bottle makes an acceptable substitute.

SIEVE OR STRAINER

You'll need a fine sieve to sift ingredients that tend to clump, such as confectioner's (icing) sugar and cocoa. Sieves can also be used to strain liquids from fruits.

PASTRY BRUSH

This is a very handy tool: not only can it be used to brush liquid glazes over warm cakes, but it's also ideal for removing excess crumbs from cakes and their serving plates before frosting.

WOODEN SPOONS

Large ones are ideal for mixing cookie dough and smaller flat ones are useful for stirring cooked mixtures.

GRATERS, ZESTERS AND PEELERS

A coarse grater is used for vegetables such as carrots and zucchini and often chocolate. A very fine grater is needed for zest. You can purchase a zester, a gadget with tiny teeth specifically designed for this purpose, at kitchen supply stores. A 4-sided grater with different-size holes, including fine, medium, coarse and one for shaving, also works well. A vegetable peeler does double duty making chocolate curls for decoration.

MEASURING CUPS AND SPOONS

Inaccurate measuring is one of the most common mistakes in baking. For information on how to measure, see page 13. It's important to use dry measuring cups, which are sold in sets, to measure dry ingredients such as flour, sugar, coconut and so on. Liquids should be measured in clear measuring cups with graduated markings. They come in a variety of sizes, ranging from 1 cup (250 mL) to 8 cups (2 L) and have a spout for easy pouring. Measuring spoons are used for both liquid and dry ingredients.

ICE CREAM SCOOPS

Ice cream scoops are useful because they help achieve uniformity in size and shape. Small ones are used for cookie dough and larger ones for muffins and cupcakes. Buy scoops that have a wire release, which removes the dough easily from the scoop.

Know Your Ingredients

CAKE MIXES

Cake mixes contain many of the same ingredients that are required to bake cakes from scratch. These include flour, sugar, leavening (baking powder and baking soda), fat, salt, flavoring and coloring. The difference is they are already measured in the correct proportion. When using a standard cake mix, you add eggs, oil and water.

Cake mixes also contain ingredients that are not in your kitchen cupboard, such as emulsifiers, conditioners and thickeners. These are added to make the mix more tolerant so it will perform well even if a consumer doesn't follow precisely the recommended measurements and method. A little water more or less, large or small eggs, more or less oil, underbeating, overbeating — all can be tolerated. Another advantage of cake mixes is that they have a shelf life of one year when stored unopened in a cool dry place. This makes it convenient to add cake mix to the list of staple ingredients you keep on hand. On my shelf at all times, I like to have two each of white, chocolate and lemon cake mixes and one each of spice and marble mixes. With this range, I am ready to make any recipe in this book.

Be aware that cake mix flavors vary considerably among manufacturers. For instance, some white mixes have a vanilla flavor, while others taste of almond. And, there are as many different chocolate tastes as there are in chocolate bars. I prefer white to yellow cake, as the flavor is not as strong. In my opinion, this makes white cake more versatile, as it can accommodate a wider range of flavors; however, this is entirely a personal preference. In most recipes, they are interchangeable. You should compare the two in a few recipes and pick your favorite.

You will also find that there are several different kinds of chocolate mixes available. Again, try a few and choose your favorite. Usually they are interchangeable and your choice will depend upon whether you prefer a stronger or milder chocolate taste.

Every recipe in this book has been tested using Duncan Hines Cake Mixes. When you start with a superior quality product, you're likely to end up with a dessert you'll be proud of.

FATS

It's important to use the type of fat specified in the recipe, as this has been used in testing. Sometimes a liquid is used (oil, melted butter) and sometimes solid fat (butter) is required.

- **Vegetable Oil:** This is the most common fat required for cake mixes. It works well with the mix ingredients to give you a light, tender moist cake. Select a light, flavorless oil such as canola, safflower, sunflower or corn rather than heavier varieties such as olive.
- **Butter or Margarine:** I prefer to use lightly salted butter in baking. It has a wonderful flavor and nice browning qualities. In most cases, hard margarine can be substituted. Do not use the soft tub type margarines or spreads as they do not have the same consistency as butter. Hard margarines work best where there are other strong flavors such as spices and chocolate and the "buttery" taste isn't as important. The exception is frostings where unsalted butter is preferred.
- **Shortening:** Think of shortening as a solid form of vegetable oil. I use it mainly for greasing pans rather than as an ingredient. Cooking sprays also work well for greasing pans. They are especially convenient for Bundt and muffin pans. Oil or butter tends to stick and burn more easily.

SUGARS

- **Granulated Sugar (White):** I use regular granulated sugar in recipe testing. It is free flowing and doesn't require sifting. You can also buy superfine, or fruit sugar, but I only use this in shortbread.
- **Confectioner's Sugar:** Also referred to as icing sugar or powdered sugar, this type of sugar has been ground to a fine powder and approximately 3% cornstarch has been added to prevent lumping and crystallization during storage. (Be sure to keep the bag airtight as it can clump when stored). Confectioner's sugar is used primarily in frostings and glazes. It dissolves almost instantly in liquids, which makes it handy for sweetening whipping cream. When using confectioner's sugar, I prefer to measure it first, then sift. I have based my recipes on this method rather than on sifting first and then measuring.
- **Brown Sugar:** This is less refined than granulated sugar. It is used mainly for toppings, streusels and some frostings. It isn't used much in cake batters as it makes them heavier and overly moist. However, these characteristics make brown sugar preferable for use in many cookies and bars which benefit from the denser texture and caramel flavor. The darker the color, the more molasses and moisture it contains, which intensifies the flavor. I like the golden variety (sometimes called yellow) for recipe testing, but light and dark are interchangeable. Because of its moisture content, brown sugar tends to lump. Store it airtight in a covered jar or heavy plastic bag in a cool dry place. If it does harden, put it in a plastic bag with a slice of apple for a few days.
- **Coarse Sugar:** This is sometimes used in toppings or to coat cookies before baking, but it should not be used in batter or dough, as it does not dissolve readily.

EGGS

Eggs contribute to leavening, texture, color, flavor, volume, richness and nutritional value in cakes. In other words, they are among the most important ingredients!

I use large eggs for all recipe testing. Remove eggs from the refrigerator at least one hour before using them so they can come to room temperature. When egg whites are to be beaten, separate the eggs when cold, then cover both whites and yolks with plastic wrap to prevent their drying out.

LIQUIDS

Water is the most common liquid used in cake mixes, but there are others.

- **Milk:** I prefer 2% milk, but homogenized, 1% and skim will also work, although recipe results will vary slightly due to the different fat content.
- **Buttermilk:** This is made from lower-fat milk and a bacterial culture. You can buy buttermilk in the dairy case or prepare your own. To make 1 cup (250 mL) buttermilk, mix 1 tbsp (15 mL) vinegar or lemon juice and enough milk to make 1 cup (250 mL); let stand 5 minutes, then stir.
- **Evaporated Milk:** Evaporating milk to half its volume makes this canned milk product. It has a mild caramel taste and comes in whole or low-fat versions.
- **Light Cream:** This has a milk fat content (M.F.) of 10% and is also called half-and-half cream.
- **Table Cream:** This has 18% M.F. and it can be used in recipes that call for light cream.
- **Whipping Cream:** Also called heavy cream, this has 35% M.F.
- **Sour Cream:** This has about 14% M.F. and is also available in lower-fat and no-fat versions. Use the regular or lower-fat kind in baking, but not no-fat. In most recipes, plain yogurt can be substituted.

- **Yogurt:** It's available in plain and flavored, with in a range of fat contents. As with sour cream, don't use the no-fat variety for baking.
- **Sweetened Condensed Milk:** This is evaporated milk that has been reduced further and sweetened. It is available in whole and lower-fat versions. All testing was done using the whole or regular variety.

NUTS

As nuts are high in fat, they tend to go rancid quickly. Store nuts in the freezer to keep them fresh. When ready to use, thaw nuts and use them as directed or, for optimum flavor, toast them first.

To toast nuts, spread them out in a single layer on a baking sheet. Bake at 350°F (180°C) for 5 to 10 minutes, stirring often until golden and fragrant. Cool before using. Chopped nuts will toast in less time than whole nuts. For hazelnuts, rub off the skins in a tea towel while warm. 1 cup (250 mL) of lightly toasted nuts is about $3\frac{1}{2}$ oz (100 g).

COCONUT

Store coconut in the freezer, as it is high in fat. Like nuts, coconut has a nicer flavor when toasted. I prefer flaked or shredded coconut rather than desiccated in baking. Sweetened or unsweetened is a matter of choice.

To toast, spread the coconut in a single layer on a baking sheet. Bake at 350°F (180°C) for about 5 minutes, stirring often until light golden. Watch carefully as coconut burns quickly.

CHOCOLATE

This is a must-have ingredient that you should never be without! Chocolate comes in a variety of forms. Keep a supply of semi-sweet or bittersweet chocolate in a cool place. Unsweetened chocolate is not used as often, but keep a small amount on hand for some of the frostings. Chocolate is chopped, grated or melted for use in recipes.

Chocolate chips are formulated to soften but still hold their shape during baking. In general, they are used in and on top of cakes while block chocolate or squares are used for melting.

White chocolate is not really chocolate but has become a popular ingredient in baking. Be sure to buy pure white chocolate, (read the label and look for "pure" or "100% pure") not the artificial kind, which won't melt properly. Cocoa is a dry, unsweetened powder made from chocolate liquor with most of the cocoa butter removed. As cocoa tends to clump on storage, it needs to be sifted before using. As with confectioner's sugar, measure first, then sift.

Melting Chocolate: Coarsely chop chocolate. Melt slowly in the top of a double boiler or a bowl set over hot — not boiling — water until almost melted. Stir to finish melting completely. Don't put a lid on the pan, as condensation will cause chocolate to seize. You can also melt chocolate in a small saucepan on low heat, stirring constantly until smooth or in a microwave oven. Place the chopped chocolate in a microwave-safe bowl, cover tightly and heat at medium power until almost melted (about 30 seconds to 1 minute per ounce (28 g) depending upon the quantity of chocolate and microwave power). Remove from oven and stir until completely melted.

To make chocolate curls, heat a block or square of chocolate in a microwave oven for 10 seconds until it is just warm but not melted. Then shave warm chocolate with a vegetable peeler. For longer curls, use a larger chunk of chocolate and increase microwave time slightly.

FLAVORINGS

Always use pure extracts, not artificial. The price is considerably more but you use less and the flavor is well worth it.

FOOD COLORS

The four basic liquid food colors are red, green, blue and yellow. They are usually sold in a kit which should meet all your decorating needs.

SPICES

Keep your favorite spices on hand. Buy them in small amounts and store in tightly sealed glass containers in a cool, dark place. Replace within 6 to 9 months.

CREAM CHEESE

I prefer full-fat cream cheese but you can substitute a lower-fat variety, if you prefer. Use the blocks of cream cheese softened to room temperature for smooth blending. Don't use the tubs of soft, spreadable cheese, which are usually whipped with the addition of liquid and therefore not the right consistency for baking.

DRIED FRUIT

Keep raisins, apricots, cranberries and dates on hand for general baking. For special holidays, purchase candied fruit. Fruit may sink if the batter is not stiff enough. Chop fruit finely and toss it in flour to coat and help suspend the pieces in the batter.

FRESH FRUIT

- **Lemons:** One medium lemon yields about $1/4$ cup (50 mL) juice and 2 tsp (10 mL) grated zest.

- **Oranges:** Two to three medium oranges yield 1 cup (250 mL) juice and 3 tbsp (45 mL) grated zest.
- **Limes:** One medium lime yields about 2 tbsp (25 mL) juice and 1 tsp (5 mL) grated zest.

    To get the most juice from citrus fruit, warm the fruit slightly in boiling water or microwave it for about 10 seconds.
- **Apples:** One pound (500 g) or three medium apples yield about 3 cups (750 mL) sliced or diced. When cutting, sprinkle the board with lemon juice then squeeze it on cut fruit to prevent discoloration.
- **Bananas:** One pound (500 g) or two to three large bananas yield 1 cup (250 mL) mashed.
- **Strawberries and Raspberries:** One pound (500 g) contains about 4 cups (1 L) whole berries, 3 cups (750 mL) sliced or 2 cups (500 mL) crushed.

CANNED FRUITS

Keep a supply of the common types of canned fruit on hand. This includes pineapple (crushed and rings), apricots, peaches, mandarin oranges and mango. Brands will vary in the proportion of liquid to solid fruit as well as in the color and size of fruit pieces.

FROZEN FRUIT

Keep a few bags of cranberries in your freezer, as they can be hard to find out of season. Buy other frozen fruits, such as rhubarb, peaches and berries as needed. In general, I prefer to use fresh fruit, if it's available.

Cake Baking Tips and Techniques

PLAN IN ADVANCE
Before you start, read the recipe carefully, checking the ingredients, utensils and equipment required, as well as the baking time.

Gather all the ingredients and equipment you need. Perform tasks such as chopping or toasting nuts, preparing fruit or grating zest. Having this out of the way ahead of time makes mixing quick and easy.

Allow adequate time to soften butter and bring cold ingredients such as eggs to room temperature.

Adjust the oven rack to the middle level for most cake baking. Angel food cakes are baked on the lower rack. Always check the cake mix package or recipe for specified directions. About 15 minutes before you plan to bake, preheat your oven.

USE THE RIGHT PAN PROPERLY PREPARED
Use the pan size recommended in the recipe and prepare pans as required. Grease lightly with shortening or a vegetable cooking spray. Don't use butter, margarine or oil, which are more likely to stick and burn. If the pan also requires flouring, sprinkle the greased surface lightly with flour. Shake to evenly distribute, then shake out any excess flour. Pans for layer cakes can also be lined with a circle of parchment paper on the bottom, which makes cake removal foolproof. For rectangular cakes that won't be served from the pan, I like to line the pan with foil, leaving an overhang. Grease the foil. The cooled cake can be removed from the pan easily using the overhang as handles. The same technique works well for bars and squares, especially those that tend to stick to the pan.

You will probably find bars and squares easier to cut after they have been removed from the pan. Lift them out of the pan in the foil and place on a cutting board. For muffins and cupcakes, paper liners can replace greasing. When using springform pans in addition to greasing, it's a good idea to place them on a piece of foil to catch drips that may leak out if the seal between the rim and the base is not perfect.

The exception is angel food cake. The pan is left ungreased so the batter crawls up, sticking to the sides as it rises during baking.

MEASURE ACCURATELY
Accuracy is very important in baking and inaccurate measuring is one of the most common mistakes. Use liquid (usually clear) measures for liquids. Read the measurement at eye level. For dry ingredients, you will need a set of graduated measures specifically intended for dry ingredients. They have a straight rim so the ingredients can be leveled off. Spoon the ingredients into the appropriate measure and level off with a straight spatula or knife. Don't tap or pack! Brown sugar requires a different technique. It is firmly packed into the cup, then leveled off. It should hold the cup shape when turned out. Unless otherwise specified, dry ingredients should be measured before sifting and butter before it is melted. Use measuring spoons for small amounts of both liquid and dry ingredients.

MIX PROPERLY
Mix batters in a large mixer bowl using an electric mixer. Start on low speed for about 1 minute, to blend liquid and dry ingredients, and prevent splattering. Then increase the speed to medium and beat for 2 minutes or until the mixture is smooth. Scrape the bowl often during mixing.

FILL PANS CAREFULLY

When baking layer cakes, it's important to divide the batter evenly between the pans so the layers are the same height and will bake evenly. If possible, use a kitchen scale to measure the weight of each filled pan. For most plain cakes, bang the pan firmly against the counter top after spreading the batter in the pan. This eliminates any large air bubbles. Don't do this with angel food cakes, marble cakes or cakes with a streusel filling or topping or a lot of fruit or nuts throughout.

BAKE IMMEDIATELY

Bake the cake as soon as it is mixed as the leavening in a mix starts to work as soon as it is moistened. A delay in baking after mixing will result in poor volume. For proper heat distribution, pans should not touch each other or the sides of the oven during baking. If your oven won't hold 3 pans on a shelf, put 2 on the upper middle rack and 1 on a lower rack. Change positions halfway through baking.

USE TIMES AS A GUIDELINE

Use the recommended baking times as a guideline. Always set your timer for 5 minutes before the minimum time given to allow for oven variances. Ovens are often hotter than the temperature indicates and cakes can easily be overdone, especially those that are high in sugar or baked in a dark pan. It's much safer to add more time in 5-minute segments if a cake needs more baking.

TEST FOR DONENESS

When cakes are done, a toothpick, wooden skewer or cake tester inserted in the center will come out clean. (A strand of spaghetti often works well, too! But not for some cakes with gooey ingredients.) Another indication that the cake is done is that the top springs back when lightly touched and the cake comes away from the sides of the pan. For lighter cakes, the color is also a good indicator — it should be a nice golden brown.

ALLOW TO COOL

Unless otherwise specified, allow layer cakes to cool in the pan for 10 minutes and deeper cakes, such as tube cakes and loaves for 20 minutes. Leave the cake in the pan on a wire rack. To remove cake from pan, run a knife around edge and center of tube pans then invert, shaking gently to remove cake. Bundt cakes are cooled initially in the pan, then turned out and left to finish cooling fluted side up. All other cakes are inverted twice so they finish cooling in the same position (top side up) as they are baked. Angel food cakes are an exception. The baked cake is immediately turned upside down on a funnel, bottle or glass bottom and left until completely cool.

GLAZE OR FROST AS YOU PREFER

Glazes are often applied while cakes are warm, while butter icings and frostings are applied after they have completely cooled. Often there is no right or wrong frosting or glaze for a cake. It really is a matter of personal preference. Keep both color and flavor in mind when deciding how to finish your cake. I've given several ideas for cake and frosting combinations in most recipes but these should be used only as a guideline. Duncan Hines offers an array of ready-to-serve frostings that are an excellent quick and easy alternative to homemade.

MORE ABOUT FINISHING CAKES

Cakes baked in 13- by 9-inch (3.5 L) pans are usually glazed or frosted and served right from the pan. Pans with lids are ideal for toting desserts to get-togethers.

When cakes are brushed with syrup while warm (usually tube and Bundt cakes), put the cake on a wire rack over waxed paper to catch the drips.

thick, pourable consistency is reached. Pour over cake and leave to harden.

Drizzle. Thin lines of white icing make a nice finish for coffee cakes. Mix confectioner's (icing) sugar with a little milk to make a thin drizzling consistency. Dip a

---

TIPS FOR FROSTING LAYER CAKES

- Brush loose crumbs from the sides of the cake.
- Freeze cakes for about 30 minutes. This makes them less fragile and easier to frost.
- If layers are domed, slice a bit off the top to even them off.
- Place the first cake layer topside down on plate.
- Spread $\frac{1}{2}$ to $\frac{3}{4}$ cup (125 to 175 mL) frosting on the cake. If the filling is a jam that may bleed into the frosting, leave a $\frac{1}{2}$-inch (2 cm) border around the edge. Place a second cake layer, topside up over frosting. You now have the two flat surfaces together in the center so the cakes will sit evenly.

- Put a bit of frosting on the serving plate, then place cake on top. This will anchor the cake in place.
- To keep the serving plate clean, set 4 strips of waxed paper, forming a square, under the edge of the cake.
- Spread a very thin layer of frosting on top and sides of cake. This seals the crumbs. Then cover with a second, thicker layer of frosting. You can smooth the surface with a long spatula or make swirls with a small spatula or the back of a spoon. The tines of a dinner fork can be used to make wave designs in frosting.
- Chill cake, if necessary, to firm up frosting. Carefully remove waxed paper strips.

Dusting with confectioner's sugar is a simple yet attractive finish for plain cakes. Do this just before serving since the moisture from the cake will quickly absorb the dusting. For an elegant or festive look, place a doily over the cake, sprinkle generously with confectioner's sugar, and then remove the doily.

Simple **garnishes** such as whole or chopped nuts, shaved chocolate and fresh fruit can also dress up cakes.

Quick glaze. Microwave a ready-to-serve frosting for about 40 seconds, or just until it is slightly warmed, then stir until a shiny,

large spoon into the icing and quickly move it back and forth over the cake. For a chocolate drizzle, melt chocolate and use a spoon or fork in a similar fashion.

STORING CAKES

Properly wrapped, cake keeps very well. You can refrigerate most cakes up to a week or freeze them 4 to 6 months.

Cool unfrosted cakes completely before freezing. Having a few plain cake layers in the freezer is a bonus. When necessary, you can thaw, fill and frost in no time.

Chill or freeze frosted cake for about 30 minutes to harden frosting so it doesn't stick to the wrapping. In general, other baked goods such as muffins, loaves, cookies and bars freeze very well. Store them in reusable plastic freezer bags so you can easily remove just the amount you require.

Avoid freezing desserts that contain a lot of cream. These are much better freshly prepared.

THAWING CAKES

Thaw frosted cakes overnight in the refrigerator, if the frosting contains eggs or cream. Thaw other cakes the same way, or at room temperature, for about 3 hours.

When unfrosted cakes are going to be frosted, leave covered about three-quarters of thawing time then uncover for the remaining time so they dry out slightly. This makes them easier to frost.

HIGH-ALTITIDE BAKING

At high altitudes, above 3,500 feet (1,000 m), there is less air pressure and humidity. Both these factors can drastically affect baking. Lower air pressure can cause cakes to overflow or collapse. Don't fill the pans more than half full with batter. It also helps to use eggs that are cold rather than the usual room temperature. You should add 2 tbsp (25 mL) extra flour to toughen the cakes a little. Increase the oven temperature by 25°F (10°C) to set the batter before it over-rises. If given a choice, use the larger pan size suggested. Cakes also tend to stick to the pans more. Be sure to grease the pans generously before dusting with flour.

Single-Layer Cakes

Peanut Butter and Banana Cake

Preheat oven to 350°F (180°C)
13- by 9-inch (3 L) cake pan, greased

SERVES 12 TO 16

A delicious cake with a taste that's reminiscent of the popular sandwich, this also makes a great addition to a lunchbox.

Tip
Buy bananas a bit green so they'll be ripe when you're ready to use them.

Variation
If you prefer a milder banana flavor, use a vanilla instant pudding mix.

1	pkg (18.25 oz/515 g) white cake mix	1
1	pkg (4-serving size) banana instant pudding mix	1
4	eggs	4
1½ cups	mashed ripe bananas (3 to 4 large bananas)	375 mL
⅓ cup	vegetable oil	75 mL
½ cup	packed brown sugar	125 mL
1½ cups	peanut butter chips	375 mL

1. In a large mixer bowl, combine cake mix, pudding mix, eggs, mashed bananas and oil. Beat on medium speed for 2 minutes. Spread half of batter in prepared pan. Sprinkle half of brown sugar and chips over batter. Repeat layers. Bake for 45 to 50 minutes or until a tester inserted in the center comes out clean. Cool completely in pan on a wire rack.

Ginger Pear Torte

Preheat oven to 350°F (180°C)
13- by 9-inch (3 L) cake pan, greased

SERVES 12 TO 16

Pear and ginger are a natural combination. The fresh gingerroot adds wonderful flavor!

Tip
Use pears that are partially ripe so they'll soften during cooking but still hold their shape.

Variation
Spicy Pear Torte:
Replace white cake with a spice cake mix and omit ground ginger in the batter.

CAKE

1	pkg (18.25 oz/515 g) white cake mix	1
1	pkg (4-serving size) vanilla instant pudding mix	1
4	eggs	4
1/2 cup	sour cream	125 mL
1/4 cup	vegetable oil	50 mL
2 tsp	finely chopped gingerroot	10 mL
1 1/2 tsp	ground ginger	7 mL
4	large pears, peeled and cored	4
2 tbsp	butter, melted	25 mL
1/3 cup	packed brown sugar	75 mL

GINGER CREAM TOPPING

1 1/2 cups	whipping (35%) cream	375 mL
3 tbsp	confectioner's (icing) sugar, sifted	45 mL
1/2 tsp	ground ginger	2 mL

1. **Cake:** In a large mixer bowl, combine cake mix, pudding mix, eggs, sour cream, oil, gingerroot and ground ginger. Beat on medium speed for 2 minutes. Spread batter evenly in prepared pan.

2. Cut pears into 1/4-inch (0.5 cm) slices. Arrange over batter, overlapping slightly as necessary. Press lightly into batter. Drizzle melted butter on top. Sprinkle brown sugar evenly over pears. Bake for 40 to 50 minutes or until set and golden. Cool in pan on a wire rack. Serve warm or cool with Ginger Cream Topping.

3. **Ginger Cream Topping:** In a large mixer bowl, combine cream, confectioner's sugar and ginger. Beat to stiff peaks. Spoon over sliced cake.

Apple Crisp Cake

Preheat oven to 350°F (180°C)
13- by 9-inch (3 L) cake pan, greased

SERVES 12 TO 16

*This cake tastes
like one of
my favorite old-
fashioned desserts,
apple crisp.*

Tips
Use apples that are
firm and tart, such
as Granny Smith,
Spies or Spartans.

Serve cake warm
with a drizzle of
caramel sauce and
a scoop of vanilla
ice cream.

Variation
Replace 1 cup
(250 mL) of the
apples with fresh
berries such as
blueberries,
raspberries or
cranberries.

TOPPING

$2/3$ cup	quick-cooking oats	150 mL
$1/2$ cup	all purpose flour	125 mL
$1/3$ cup	packed brown sugar	75 mL
$1/2$ tsp	ground cinnamon	2 mL
$1/2$ cup	butter	125 mL

CAKE

1	pkg (18.25 oz/515 g) white cake mix	1
3	eggs	3
1 cup	water	250 mL
$1/2$ cup	butter, softened	125 mL
1 tsp	ground cinnamon	5 mL
$2^1/2$ cups	thinly sliced apples (3 large apples)	625 mL

1. *Topping:* In a bowl, combine oats, flour, brown sugar
   and cinnamon. Cut in butter with pastry blender or fork
   until crumbly. Set aside.

2. *Cake:* In a large mixer bowl, combine cake mix, eggs,
   water, butter and cinnamon. Beat on medium speed
   for 2 minutes. Spread batter evenly in prepared pan.
   Arrange apple slices evenly over batter. Sprinkle topping
   over apples. Bake for 40 to 45 minutes or until a tester
   inserted in the center comes out clean. Cool completely
   in pan on a wire rack.

Pretty Pistachio Cake

Preheat oven to 350°F (180°C)
13- by 9-inch (3 L) cake pan, greased

SERVES 12 TO 16

The green color can be as subtle or as bright as you like, depending upon the amount of green food coloring you add. Either way, the delicate flavor is a favorite.

Tip
For a different look, bake this in a tube pan for 1 hour or in 2 (9-inch/23 cm) round pans for 30 minutes. Put the topping between and on top of the layers.

Variation
Replace whipped topping with 1 cup (250 mL) whipping (35%) cream beaten to stiff peaks.

CAKE

1	pkg (18.25 oz/515 g) white cake mix	1
1	pkg (4-serving size) pistachio instant pudding mix	1
4	eggs	4
1 cup	water	250 mL
2/3 cup	vegetable oil	150 mL
3	drops green food coloring, optional	3

PISTACHIO CREAM TOPPING

1	pkg (4-serving size) pistachio instant pudding mix	1
1 cup	milk	250 mL
1 1/2 cups	frozen whipped topping, thawed	375 mL
	Chopped pistachio nuts, optional	

1. **Cake:** In a large mixer bowl, combine cake mix, pudding mix, eggs, water and oil. Beat on medium speed for 2 minutes. Stir in coloring, if desired. Spread batter evenly in prepared pan. Bake for 35 to 40 minutes or until a tester inserted in the center comes out clean. Cool completely in pan on a wire rack.

2. **Topping:** In a large mixer bowl, combine pudding mix and milk. Beat on low speed for 1 minute. Let set for 2 minutes. Add whipped topping. Beat on low speed just to blend. Spread over cooled cake. Sprinkle with chopped pistachios, if desired. Chill until serving. Store leftover cake in the refrigerator.

21

Banana Cake

Preheat oven to 350°F (180°C)
13- by 9-inch (3 L) cake pan, greased

SERVES 12 TO 16

This cake is delicious with a frosting such as Banana Butter Frosting (page 179), but it's also scrumptious served warm, topped with vanilla ice cream and a drizzle of caramel sauce.

1	pkg (18.25 oz/515 g) white cake mix	1
3	eggs	3
1²⁄₃ cups	mashed ripe bananas (3 to 4 large bananas)	400 mL
1⁄₃ cup	vegetable oil	75 mL

1. In a large mixer bowl, combine cake mix, eggs, bananas and oil. Beat on medium speed for 2 minutes or until smooth. Spread batter evenly in prepared pan. Bake for 35 to 40 minutes or until a tester inserted in the center comes out clean. Cool completely in pan on a wire rack. Frost as desired.

Dump Cake

Preheat oven to 350°F (180°C)
13- by 9-inch (3 L) cake pan, greased

SERVES 12 TO 16

As the name implies, the ingredients for this delicious and easy-to-make cake are dumped into the pan in order.

Tip
When baking in glass or dark metal pans, reduce your oven temperature by 25°F (10°C).

1	can (19 oz/540 mL) crushed pineapple, including juice	1
1	can (19 oz/540 mL) cherry pie filling	1
1	pkg (18.25 oz/515 g) yellow cake mix	1
1 cup	coarsely chopped almonds	250 mL
2⁄₃ cup	butter, cut in thin slices	150 mL

1. Dump pineapple, including juice in prepared pan. Spread evenly. Spoon pie filling evenly over top. Sprinkle cake mix evenly over fruit. Sprinkle nuts on top. Put butter over nuts, covering as much as possible. Bake for 45 to 55 minutes or until golden. Serve warm or cool.

Old-Fashioned Apple Nut Cake

Preheat oven to 350°F (180°C)
13- by 9-inch (3 L) cake pan, greased

SERVES 12 TO 16

The apple pie filling produces a moist, flavorful cake that keeps well.

Tip
If the apple pie filling is coarsely chopped first using a food processor or potato masher, it makes the cake easy to slice.

Variation
Try a yellow cake mix in place of the white.

CAKE

1	can (19 oz/540 mL) apple pie filling	1
1	pkg (18.25 oz/515 g) white cake mix	1
1/2 cup	all-purpose flour	125 mL
1 tsp	baking powder	5 mL
3	eggs	3
1/2 cup	vegetable oil	125 mL

TOPPING

1/2 cup	packed brown sugar	125 mL
1/2 cup	all-purpose flour	125 mL
1 tsp	ground cinnamon	5 mL
1/4 cup	butter, softened	50 mL
1/2 cup	chopped nuts	125 mL

1. **Cake:** Process apple pie filling in food processor or with a potato masher until coarsely chopped. In a large mixer bowl, combine pie filling, cake mix, flour, baking powder, eggs and oil. Beat on medium speed for 2 minutes. Spread batter evenly in prepared pan.

2. **Topping:** In a bowl, combine brown sugar, flour and cinnamon. Cut in butter with pastry blender or fork until crumbly. Stir in nuts. Sprinkle evenly over batter. Bake for 40 to 50 minutes or until a tester inserted in the center comes out clean. Let cool in pan on a wire rack for at least 30 minutes before cutting.

Peach Melba Upside-Down Cake

Preheat oven to 350°F (180°C)
13- by 9-inch (3 L) cake pan

SERVES 12 TO 16

Canned peaches are a good choice for upside-down cakes, as they keep their color and texture during baking.

Tip
If you want evenly sized slices, buy peach halves and slice them yourself. For convenience, pre-sliced peaches work well.

Variation
Replace raspberries with ¹/₂ cup (125 mL) maraschino cherry halves.

¹/₃ cup	butter	75 mL
1 cup	packed brown sugar	250 mL
1	can (28 oz/796 mL) sliced peaches	1
	Water	
1 cup	fresh raspberries	250 mL
1	pkg (18.25 oz/515 g) white cake mix	1
2	eggs	2
3 tbsp	vegetable oil	45 mL
	Whipped cream, optional	

1. Melt butter in cake pan. Sprinkle brown sugar evenly on top.

2. Drain peaches, reserving peach syrup. Add water to syrup to make 1¹/₃ cups (325 mL) liquid; set aside. Arrange peach slices over brown sugar mixture. Scatter raspberries on top.

3. In a large mixer bowl, combine peach syrup mixture, cake mix, eggs and oil. Beat on medium speed for 2 minutes. Pour batter evenly over fruit. Bake for 45 to 50 minutes or until a tester inserted in the center comes out clean. Let cool in pan on a wire rack for 5 minutes, then turn upside-down onto a large platter or cookie sheet. Serve warm with a generous dollop of whipped cream, if desired.

Spice Cake with Cinnamon Butter Frosting

Preheat oven to 350°F (180°C)
13- by 9-inch (3 L) cake pan, greased

SERVES 12 TO 16

Here's a quick and delicious way to make spice cake from a white cake mix.

Tips
This cake is very light and tender. The addition of raisins or other fruit doesn't work well as the batter isn't strong enough to support them. They will sink, creating a layer of fruit on the bottom of the cake.

This is my favorite blend of spices but you can adjust the spices to suit your taste.

1	pkg (18.25 oz/515 g) white cake mix	1
2½ tsp	ground cinnamon	12 mL
¾ tsp	ground nutmeg	4 mL
¼ tsp	ground cloves	1 mL
3	eggs	3
1⅓ cups	water	325 mL
⅓ cup	vegetable oil	75 mL
	Cinnamon Butter Frosting (see recipe, page 173)	

1. In a large mixer bowl, combine cake mix, cinnamon, nutmeg, cloves, eggs, water and oil. Beat on medium speed for 2 minutes. Spread batter evenly in prepared pan. Bake for 35 to 40 minutes or until a tester inserted in the center comes out clean. Cool completely in pan on a wire rack. Frost with Cinnamon Butter Frosting or as desired.

Butterscotch Chip Cake

Preheat oven to 350°F (180°C)
13- by 9-inch (3 L) cake pan, greased

SERVES 12 TO 16

The double dose of butterscotch in this cake is as good as candy.

Tip
Scatter the chips on the cake batter before adding the nuts. They'll sink during baking, creating a tempting pebbled top.

Variation
Replace butterscotch chips with milk chocolate or white chocolate chips.

1	pkg (4-serving size) butterscotch instant pudding mix	1
1²/₃ cups	milk	400 mL
1	pkg (18.25 oz/515 g) white cake mix	1
1²/₃ cups	butterscotch chips (10 oz/300 g pkg)	400 mL
1¹/₄ cups	chopped pecans	300 mL

1. In a large mixer bowl, combine pudding mix and milk. Beat on low speed for 2 minutes. Add cake mix and beat on low speed for 1 minute longer or until smooth. Spread batter in prepared pan. Scatter butterscotch chips and then pecans on top. Bake for 35 to 45 minutes or until a tester inserted in the center comes out clean. Let cool in pan on a wire rack for at least 30 minutes before cutting.

Chocolate Nut Carrot Cake

Preheat oven to 350°F (180°C)
13- by 9-inch (3 L) cake pan, greased

SERVES 12 TO 16

Two favorite cakes, chocolate and carrot, are combined in this rich and tasty dessert.

Tips

In this recipe, use block cream cheese at room temperature, not tubs of spreadable cream cheese.

For a double hit of chocolate, finish this cake with Chocolate Cream Cheese Frosting. Sprinkle with finely chopped nuts or shaved chocolate and decorate with small candied carrots.

1	pkg (18.25 oz/515 g) devil's food cake mix	1
4 oz	cream cheese, softened	125 g
1/4 cup	granulated sugar	50 mL
3	eggs	3
1/3 cup	water	75 mL
1 tsp	ground cinnamon	5 mL
1/4 tsp	ground cloves	1 mL
2 1/2 cups	grated peeled carrots	625 mL
2/3 cup	finely chopped nuts	150 mL
	Chocolate Cream Cheese Frosting (see recipe, page 178) or Basic Cream Cheese Frosting (see recipe, page 171)	

1. In a large mixer bowl, combine cake mix, cream cheese, sugar, eggs, water, cinnamon and cloves. Beat on low speed for 1 minute, then on medium speed for 2 minutes or until smooth. Stir in carrots and nuts. Spread batter evenly in prepared pan. Bake for 40 to 50 minutes or until a tester inserted in the center comes out clean. Cool completely in pan on a wire rack. Frost and decorate as desired.

Chocolate Chip 'n' Nut Cake

Preheat oven to 350°F (180°C)
13- by 9-inch (3 L) cake pan, greased

SERVES 12 TO 16

This one-step cake has the topping baked right on. No need to cool and frost later.

Tip
Cakes made with sour cream or yogurt are generally moist and keep well.

Variation
For a nice change, try using milk chocolate chips instead of semi-sweet.

1	pkg (18.25 oz/515 g) devil's food cake mix	1
1	pkg (4-serving size) chocolate instant pudding mix	1
4	eggs	4
1 cup	sour cream	250 mL
1/2 cup	vegetable oil	125 mL
1/3 cup	water	75 mL
2 cups	miniature semi-sweet chocolate chips, divided	500 mL
1/2 cup	chopped nuts, optional	125 mL

1. In a large mixer bowl, combine cake mix, pudding mix, eggs, sour cream, oil and water. Beat on medium speed for 2 minutes or until smooth. Stir in 1 1/4 cups (300 mL) of the chocolate chips. Spread batter evenly in prepared pan. Sprinkle remaining chocolate chips and nuts evenly over batter. Bake for 45 to 50 minutes or until a tester inserted in the center comes out clean. Let cool in pan on a wire rack for at least 30 minutes before cutting.

Chocolate Caramel Pecan Cake

Preheat oven to 350°F (180°C)
13- by 9-inch (3 L) cake pan, greased

SERVES 12 TO 16

Here's a cake version of the favorite chocolate caramel pecan candy. Every mouthful is wonderfully gooey, nutty and decadent.

Tip
Be sure to stir the filling constantly while cooking, as it burns easily.

Variation
To make a quick caramel filling, omit brown sugar and corn syrup, decrease butter to ½ cup (125 mL), increase sweetened condensed milk to 1 can (10 oz/300 mL). Add 75 soft caramels (20 oz/600 g). Heat in a saucepan over medium heat, stirring until caramels are melted and mixture is smooth.

FILLING & TOPPING

1 cup	butter	250 mL
1 cup	packed brown sugar	250 mL
1 cup	sweetened condensed milk	250 mL
¼ cup	corn syrup	50 mL
1 cup	milk chocolate chips or miniature semi-sweet chocolate chips	250 mL
2 cups	finely chopped pecans, divided	500 mL

CAKE

1	pkg (18.25 oz/515 g) devil's food cake mix	1
3	eggs	3
1¼ cups	water	300 mL
⅓ cup	vegetable oil	75 mL

1. **Filling:** In a heavy saucepan, combine butter, brown sugar, sweetened condensed milk and corn syrup. Cook over medium heat, stirring constantly until mixture comes to a boil, then simmer for 5 minutes. Keep warm over a bowl of hot water, stirring occasionally, while preparing cake.

2. **Cake:** In a large mixer bowl, combine cake mix, eggs, water and oil. Beat at medium speed for 2 minutes. Spread half of batter in prepared pan. Bake for 15 minutes or until the center of the cake is set. Remove from oven.

3. **Topping:** Pour warm caramel mixture evenly over baked cake. Sprinkle chocolate chips and 1 cup (250 mL) of the pecans on top. Spread remaining cake batter carefully over caramel layer. Sprinkle remaining pecans on top. Bake for 25 to 35 minutes longer or until the cake springs back when lightly touched. Cool completely in pan on a wire rack.

29

Cookies 'n' Cream Cake

Preheat oven to 350°F (180°C)
13- by 9-inch (3 L) cake pan, greased

SERVES 12 TO 16

Chocolate sandwich cookies are a perennial favorite. Now, kids young and old can enjoy their best-loved cookie in a cake.

Tips
To quickly chop cookies, place 6 in a food processor. Pulse several times to coarsely chop. Repeat with remaining cookies. Don't process too finely or the cake will be browner.

Cake can be cut in half horizontally and filled with frosting, if desired.

Variation
A chocolate cake mix doesn't look as good but it tastes great.

CAKE

1	pkg (18.25 oz/515 g) white cake mix	1
3	eggs	3
1⅓ cups	water	325 mL
⅓ cup	vegetable oil	75 mL
1 cup	coarsely chopped cream-filled chocolate sandwich cookies, about 12 (2½-inch/6 cm) cookies	250 mL

FROSTING

1	container (15 oz/450 g) ready-made vanilla frosting	1
⅓ cup	coarsely chopped cream-filled chocolate sandwich cookies, about 12 (2½-inch/6 cm) cookies	75 mL
	Cookies, regular or minis, to garnish	

1. **Cake:** In a large mixer bowl, combine cake mix, eggs, water and oil. Beat on medium speed 2 minutes. Stir in chopped cookies. Spread batter evenly in prepared pan. Bake for 30 to 35 minutes or until a tester inserted in the center comes out clean. Cool completely in pan on a wire rack.

2. **Frosting:** Stir chopped cookies into frosting. Spread over cooled cake. Garnish with cookies.

Coconut Pecan Cake with Coconut Pecan Cream Cheese Frosting

Preheat oven to 350°F (180°C)
13- by 9-inch (3 L) cake pan, greased

SERVES 12 TO 16

This cake is proof that with just a few everyday ingredients, you can make a spectacular dessert.

Tip
Make this cake a day ahead to let flavors mellow.

Variation
Unblanched almonds or hazelnuts are also nice.

CAKE

1	pkg (18.25 oz/515 g) white cake mix	1
1	pkg (4-serving size) vanilla instant pudding mix	1
4	eggs	4
1 cup	sour cream	250 mL
$\frac{1}{2}$ cup	vegetable oil	125 mL
$1\frac{1}{2}$ cups	flaked coconut	375 mL
$\frac{3}{4}$ cup	chopped pecans	175 mL

FROSTING

8 oz	cream cheese, softened	250 g
$\frac{1}{2}$ cup	butter, softened	125 mL
4 cups	confectioner's (icing) sugar, sifted	1 L
1 tsp	vanilla	5 mL
$\frac{2}{3}$ cup	chopped pecans	150 mL
$\frac{1}{3}$ cup	flaked coconut, toasted	75 mL

1. **Cake:** In a large mixer bowl, combine cake mix, pudding mix, eggs, sour cream and oil. Beat on medium speed for 2 minutes. Stir in coconut and pecans. Mix well. Spread batter evenly in prepared pan. Bake for 45 to 55 minutes or until a tester inserted in the center comes out clean. Cool completely in pan on a wire rack.

2. **Frosting:** In a large mixer bowl, beat cream cheese and butter until smooth. Gradually add confectioner's sugar on low speed, mixing until smooth and creamy. Add vanilla, pecans and coconut. Mix well. Spread over cooled cake. Chill until serving. Store leftover cake in the refrigerator.

Triple Chocolate Cake

Preheat oven to 350°F (180°C)
13- by 9-inch (3 L) cake pan, greased

SERVES 12 TO 16

Although this cake is easy to make, with three layers of chocolate, it's a special treat.

Tips
To make chocolate curls, warm a chunk of chocolate slightly. Using a sharp vegetable peeler and, holding the chocolate in several layers of paper towelling to prevent its melting, pull the blade toward you.

See page 11 for instructions on how to melt chocolate.

Variation
Use milk chocolate instead of semi-sweet chips in the filling.

CAKE

1	pkg (18.25 oz/515 g) white cake mix	1
2	eggs	2
1¼ cups	water	300 mL
⅓ cup	vegetable oil	75 mL
3 oz	white chocolate, melted	90 g

FILLING

1½ cups	semi-sweet chocolate chips	375 mL
¼ cup	butter	50 mL
¼ cup	corn syrup	50 mL
¼ cup	confectioner's (icing) sugar	50 mL

FROSTING

1	container (15 oz/450 g) ready-to-serve vanilla frosting	1
3 oz	white chocolate, melted	90 g
4 cups	frozen whipped topping, thawed	1 L
	Chocolate curls to garnish, optional	

1. **Cake:** In a large mixer bowl, combine cake mix, eggs, water and oil. Beat on medium speed for 2 minutes. Gradually beat in melted chocolate. Spread batter evenly in prepared pan. Bake for 35 to 40 minutes or until a tester inserted in the center comes out clean. Cool 10 minutes in pan on a wire rack.

2. **Filling:** In a small saucepan, combine chocolate chips and butter. Heat over low heat, stirring constantly until smoothly melted. Stir in syrup and confectioner's sugar. Mix well. Spread over warm cake. Cool completely.

3. **Frosting:** In a large mixer bowl, beat frosting and melted white chocolate until smooth and creamy. Fold in whipped topping. Spread over filling. Garnish with chocolate curls, if desired. Chill until serving. Store leftover cake in the refrigerator.

Apple Crisp Cake *(page 20)* ▶

Bumbleberry Cake

Preheat oven to 350°F (180°C)
13- by 9-inch (3 L) cake pan, greased

SERVES 12 TO 16

This is a great cake to make during berry season. A mixture of fresh berries nestles between a tender, light cake and a cinnamon-sugar top.

Tips
Bumbleberry is a mix of different berries, often with apples.

Choose your favorite mixture of berries or vary the taste to accommodate the season.

In baking, always use block cream cheese at room temperature, not tubs of spreadable cream cheese

Variation
If you prefer, use granulated sugar instead of brown sugar in the topping.

CAKE

1	pkg (18.25 oz/515 g) white cake mix	1
⅓ cup	granulated sugar	75 mL
8 oz	cream cheese, softened	250 g
3	eggs	3
½ cup	vegetable oil	125 mL
¼ cup	water	50 mL
1 cup	fresh blueberries	250 mL
1 cup	fresh raspberries	250 mL
1 cup	fresh blackberries	250 mL

TOPPING

¾ cup	packed brown sugar	175 mL
⅔ cup	all-purpose flour	150 mL
1 tsp	ground cinnamon	5 mL
⅓ cup	butter	75 mL

1. **Cake:** In a large mixer bowl, combine cake mix, sugar, cream cheese, eggs, oil and water. Beat on low speed for 1 minute to blend, then on medium speed for 2 minutes. Spread half of batter in prepared pan. Sprinkle berries on top. Carefully spread remaining batter over berries.

2. **Topping:** In a small bowl, combine brown sugar, flour and cinnamon. Cut in butter with pastry blender or two knives until mixture is crumbly. Sprinkle over batter. Bake for 55 to 60 minutes or until a tester inserted in the center comes out clean. Let cool in pan on a wire rack for at least 30 minutes before cutting. Serve warm or cool.

◀ Coconut Walnut Carrot Cake (*page 51*)

Chocolate Strawberry Cream Cake

Preheat oven to 350°F (180°C)
13- by 9-inch (3 L) cake pan, greased

SERVES 12 TO 16

This is a great dessert for a family get-together, as you can make it ahead of time.

Tips
Allow at least 4 hours or overnight before serving to let flavors and texture mellow.

Use a thawed frozen cream topping in place of whipped cream for convenience.

Variation
Substitute raspberries for the strawberries.

CAKE

1	pkg (18.25 oz/515 g) devil's food cake mix	1
3	eggs	3
1⅓ cups	milk	325 mL
½ cup	vegetable oil	125 mL

TOPPING

1	pkg (10 oz/284 g) frozen sweetened sliced strawberries, thawed	1
1	pkg (4-serving size) vanilla instant pudding mix	1
1 cup	milk	250 mL
1 cup	whipping (35%) cream	250 mL
	Fresh strawberries	

1. **Cake:** In a large mixer bowl, combine cake mix, eggs, milk and oil. Beat on medium speed for 2 minutes. Spread batter in prepared pan. Bake for 30 to 40 minutes or until a tester inserted in the center comes out clean. Cool completely in pan on a wire rack.

2. **Topping:** Purée frozen strawberries with syrup in a blender or food processor. Poke holes 1 inch (2.5 cm) apart on top of cooled cake using handle of wooden spoon. Spoon strawberry purée over top of cake letting it soak into the holes.

3. In a large mixer bowl, combine pudding mix and milk. Beat on low speed for 2 minutes. Chill 5 minutes to thicken. Beat cream in a separate bowl to stiff peaks. Fold into pudding mixture, gently but thoroughly. Spread over cake. Garnish with fresh strawberries. Chill 4 hours or overnight before serving. Store leftover cake in refrigerator.

Chocolate Zucchini Cake with Cranberries

Preheat oven to 350°F (180°C)
13- by 9-inch (3 L) cake pan, greased

SERVES 12 TO 16

Here's a great way to use up zucchini, which often is so abundant during the summer.

Tips

Choose small tender zucchinis and don't peel them. The green flecks are attractive in this cake.

This cake works well with a cream cheese frosting. Chocolate Cream Cheese Frosting (see recipe, page 178) is particularly nice.

Variation

Try dried cherries in place of cranberries.

1	pkg (18.25 oz/515 g) devil's food cake mix	1
1	pkg (4-serving size) chocolate instant pudding mix	1
4	eggs	4
2½ cups	grated zucchini	625 mL
⅓ cup	vegetable oil	75 mL
¼ cup	water	50 mL
1 tsp	ground cinnamon	5 mL
¼ tsp	ground nutmeg	1 mL
1 cup	dried cranberries	250 mL

1. In a large mixer bowl, combine cake mix, pudding mix, eggs, zucchini, oil, water, cinnamon and nutmeg. Beat on low speed for 1 minute to blend, then on medium speed for 2 minutes. Stir in cranberries. Spread batter in prepared pan. Bake for 40 to 45 minutes or until a tester inserted in the center comes out clean. Cool completely in pan on a wire rack. Frost as desired.

Apricot Coconut Cake

Preheat oven to 350°F (180°C)
13- by 9-inch (3 L) cake pan, greased

SERVES 12 TO 16

This delicious cake doesn't even need a frosting — it bakes right along with the cake.

Tips
If serving this cake for dessert, cut into large squares and top with ice cream. For afternoon tea, serve as small squares.

If you don't have a large rectangular serving plate, use a tray, cookie sheet or cake board. You can buy cake boards in many bulk stores.

Variation
Replace apricot jam with marmalade and apricot nectar with orange juice.

1 1/2 cups	apricot jam	375 mL
1 cup	flaked coconut	250 mL
1/4 cup	butter, melted	50 mL
1	pkg (18.25 oz/515 g) white cake mix	1
3	eggs	3
2/3 cup	apricot nectar	150 mL
2/3 cup	water	150 mL
1/3 cup	vegetable oil	75 mL

1. In a bowl, combine jam, coconut and melted butter. Mix well. Spread evenly in prepared pan.

2. In a large mixer bowl, combine cake mix, eggs, nectar, water and oil. Beat on medium speed for 2 minutes. Pour batter over jam mixture. Bake for 35 to 45 minutes or until a tester inserted in the center comes out clean. Let cool in pan for 30 minutes, then turn upside-down onto a large serving plate.

Upside-Down German Chocolate Cake

Preheat oven to 350°F (180°C)
13- by 9-inch (3 L) cake pan, greased

SERVES 12 TO 16

The creamy top on this cake sinks during baking, then reverses to the top when served.

Tips
Don't worry if the top of the cake cracks during baking. It becomes the bottom when served.

Serve with a dollop of whipped cream.

Variation
Replace some of the pecans and coconut with dried cherries.

1 ½ cups	flaked coconut	375 mL
1 ½ cups	chopped pecans	375 mL
1	pkg (18.25 oz/515 g) devil's food cake mix	1
3	eggs	3
1 ⅓ cups	water	325 mL
½ cup	vegetable oil	125 mL
8 oz	cream cheese, softened	250 g
½ cup	butter, melted and cooled	125 mL
3 ½ cups	confectioner's (icing) sugar, sifted	875 mL
	Whipped cream, optional	

1. Sprinkle coconut and pecans evenly on bottom of prepared pan. Prepare cake mix with eggs, water and oil as directed on package. Pour batter over coconut and pecans.

2. In a large mixer bowl, beat cream cheese and melted butter on low speed until creamy. Gradually add confectioner's sugar, beating until smooth. Drop by spoonfuls over cake batter. Bake for 50 to 60 minutes or until a tester inserted halfway to bottom of cake comes out clean. Cool completely in pan.

3. *To serve:* Cut into serving-size pieces; turn upside-down onto plate. Serve with whipped cream, if desired.

Ginger Applesauce Spice Cake

Preheat oven to 350°F (180°C)
10-inch (25 cm) springform pan, greased and floured

SERVES 12 TO 16

The Ginger Cream is particularly good. Don't limit its use to this cake. Try spooning it over fresh fruit.

Tip
Look for crystalized ginger that is soft. It gets hard with age.

Variations
Add ¼ cup (50 mL) minced, peeled gingerroot to batter to satisfy real ginger lovers.

Fold 3 tbsp (45 mL) finely chopped crystalized ginger into the Ginger Cream.

CAKE

1	pkg (18.25 oz/515 g) spice cake mix	1
3	eggs	3
1⅓ cups	unsweetened applesauce	325 mL
½ cup	butter, softened	125 mL
⅔ cup	chopped walnuts	150 mL
½ cup	finely chopped crystallized ginger	125 mL
	Confectioner's (icing) sugar	

GINGER CREAM

½ cup	granulated sugar	125 mL
½ cup	water	125 mL
1	piece (2 inches/5 cm) gingerroot, thinly sliced	1
1 cup	whipping (35%) cream	250 mL
1 tbsp	confectioner's (icing) sugar	15 mL

1. **Cake:** In a large mixer bowl, combine cake mix, eggs, applesauce and butter. Beat on medium speed for 2 minutes. Stir in walnuts and ginger. Spread batter in prepared pan. Bake for 55 to 60 minutes or until a tester inserted in the center comes out clean. Let cool in pan on a wire rack for 15 minutes. Remove pan sides. Cool completely.

2. **Ginger Cream:** In a small saucepan, combine granulated sugar, water and ginger. Bring to a boil, stirring until sugar dissolves, then simmer over medium heat until syrupy, about 8 minutes. Strain into a bowl and refrigerate syrup until cold. Discard ginger. In a large mixer bowl, beat cream and confectioner's sugar to soft peaks. Fold in chilled syrup.

3. **To serve:** Cut into wedges and serve with a dollop of Ginger Cream.

Multi-Layer Cakes

Triple Raspberry Treat

Preheat oven to 350°F (180°C)
Three 8-inch (20 cm) or 9-inch (23 cm) round cake pans, greased and floured

SERVES 12 TO 16

With three layers of raspberries, this cake is a real treat.

Tips
Although raspberry liqueur is expensive, the flavor is so intense that a little goes a long way.

Use homemade jam, if it's available, as it has a more intense fruit taste.

Don't use the "light" jams or fruit spreads in this recipe, as the consistency is too soft.

Variation
Replace raspberry liqueur and jam with strawberry liqueur and jam and garnish with fresh strawberries.

CAKE

1	pkg (18.25 oz/515 g) white cake mix	1
3	eggs	3
1 cup	water	250 mL
1/3 cup	raspberry liqueur	75 mL
1/3 cup	vegetable oil	75 mL

FILLING & FROSTING

1 cup	butter, softened	250 mL
4 cups	confectioner's (icing) sugar, sifted	1 L
1/3 cup	raspberry liqueur	75 mL
1/4 cup	light (10%) cream	50 mL
1 cup	raspberry jam, divided	250 mL
	Fresh raspberries to garnish, optional	

1. **Cake:** In a large mixer bowl, combine cake mix, eggs, water, liqueur and oil. Beat on medium speed for 2 minutes. Spread batter in prepared pans, dividing evenly. Bake for 20 to 25 minutes or until a tester inserted in the center comes out clean. Cool 10 minutes in pans on a wire rack, then remove and cool completely on rack. With a long sharp knife, cut each layer horizontally in half to make 6 layers.

2. **Filling & Frosting:** In a large mixer bowl, beat butter until creamy. Gradually add confectioner's sugar, liqueur and cream, beating until smooth.

3. **Assembly:** Place 1 cake layer, cut-side up, on a serving plate. Spread with 1/3 cup (75 mL) of the jam. Top with another layer, cut-side down. Spread with 1/2 cup (125 mL) of the frosting. Repeat with remaining layers, jam and frosting, ending with a cake layer, cut-side down. Frost top and sides of cake with remaining frosting. If desired, pipe some frosting on top of cake for an attractive finish. Garnish with fresh berries. Store in refrigerator.

Mandarin Cake

Preheat oven to 350°F (180°C)
Two 9-inch (23 cm) round cake pans, greased and floured

SERVES 10 TO 12

This tropical treat combines mandarin oranges, pineapple and coconut for a refreshing and delicious taste.

Tips
For better flavor and a crunchy texture, toast the coconut. Spread it on a baking sheet and bake at 350°F (180°C) for 5 to 10 minutes, stirring often until golden. Cool before using in recipes.

Brushing fruit syrup from canned fruit over warm cakes keeps them moist. Pierce the top of the cake with a fork or a tester before brushing to help syrup soak in.

Variation
Pineapple Cream Cheese Frosting (see recipe, page 171) works well on this cake. Garnish with toasted coconut.

CAKE

1	pkg (18.25 oz/515 g) white cake mix	1
1	can (10 oz/284 mL) mandarin oranges, including juice	1
4	eggs	4
¾ cup	butter, melted	175 mL
⅓ cup	pineapple juice (drained from pineapple in frosting)	75 mL

PINEAPPLE COCONUT CREAM FILLING & TOPPING

4 cups	frozen whipped topping, thawed	1 L
1	pkg (4-serving size) vanilla instant pudding mix	1
¾ cup	toasted coconut	175 mL
⅔ cup	well-drained crushed pineapple	150 mL

1. **Cake:** In a large mixer bowl, combine cake mix, mandarin oranges (including liquid), eggs and melted butter. Beat on medium speed for 2 minutes or until smooth. Spread batter in prepared pans, dividing evenly. Bake for 30 to 35 minutes or until a tester inserted in the center comes out clean. Cool 10 minutes in pans on a wire rack, then remove and cool completely on rack. Pierce top of cakes with a fork or a tester. Brush warm cakes with pineapple juice, letting it soak in. Cool completely.

2. **Filling & Topping:** In a large bowl, combine whipped topping and pudding mix. Mix gently until well blended. Fold in coconut and pineapple.

3. **Assembly:** Place 1 cake layer, top-side down on serving plate. Cover with a generous layer, about 1½ cups (375 mL) of the topping. Place remaining cake, top-side up over filling. Cover top and sides of cake with remaining topping. Chill until serving. Store leftover cake in the refrigerator.

Chocolate Peanut Butter Tower

Preheat oven to 350°F (180°C)
Two 9-inch (23 cm) round cake pans, greased and floured

SERVES 12 TO 16

Here's a showstopper of a cake that will dazzle your friends.

Tips
For smooth, easy-to-spread frostings, use creamy peanut butter rather than the chunky variety.

Don't be surprised by this batter — it is very thick.

Variation
For convenience, make a double quantity of one type of frosting instead of two different kinds.

CAKE

1	pkg (18.25 oz/515 g) devil's food cake mix	1
1	pkg (4-serving size) chocolate instant pudding mix	1
4	eggs	4
1 cup	sour cream	250 mL
1/2 cup	water	125 mL
1 cup	peanut butter chips	250 mL

PEANUT BUTTER CREAM CHEESE FROSTING

8 oz	cream cheese, softened	250 g
1/2 cup	creamy peanut butter	125 mL
4 cups	confectioner's (icing) sugar, sifted	1 L
1/4 cup	whipping (35%) cream	50 mL

CHOCOLATE CREAM CHEESE FROSTING

8 oz	cream cheese, softened	250 g
1/2 cup	butter, softened	125 mL
3 1/2 cups	confectioner's (icing) sugar, sifted	825 mL
1/3 cup	unsweetened cocoa powder, sifted	75 mL
1/4 cup	whipping (35%) cream	50 mL

TOPPING

1 cup	chopped chocolate peanut butter cups (8 oz/250 g), divided	250 mL
3/4 cup	finely chopped roasted peanuts	175 mL

1. **Cake:** In a large mixer bowl, combine cake mix, pudding mix, eggs, sour cream and water. Beat on low speed for 1 minute to blend, then on medium speed for 2 minutes. Stir in peanut butter chips. Spread batter in prepared pans, dividing evenly. Bake for 40 to 45 minutes or until a tester inserted in the center comes out clean. Cool 10 minutes in pans on a wire rack, then remove and cool completely on rack. With a long sharp knife, cut each cake horizontally in half to make 4 layers.

2. **Peanut Butter Cream Cheese Frosting:** In a large mixer bowl, beat cream cheese and peanut butter until light and fluffy. Gradually add confectioner's sugar and whipping cream, beating until smooth.

3. **Chocolate Cream Cheese Frosting:** In a large mixer bowl, beat cream cheese and butter until light and fluffy. Gradually add confectioner's sugar, cocoa and whipping cream, beating until smooth.

4. **Assembly:** Place one cake layer, cut-side up on serving plate. Spread with ¾ cup (175 mL) of the peanut butter frosting. Sprinkle ¼ cup (50 mL) of the chopped peanut butter cups on top. Repeat with remaining cake layers, peanut butter frosting and peanut butter cups. Spread chocolate frosting on sides of cake. Pipe rosettes of chocolate frosting around the top edge of cake. Press chopped peanuts on side of cake. Store in the refrigerator.

Pralines 'n' Cream Pecan Cake

Preheat oven to 350°F (180°C)
Two 9-inch (23 cm) round cake pans, greased and floured
Rimmed baking sheet, greased

SERVES 12 TO 16

If pralines 'n' cream is your favorite ice cream, here's a way to enjoy the flavor in a cake. The presentation is a knockout.

Tips
Make an extra batch of praline for munching on or your cake could be bare!

Prepare pecan praline topping up to 3 days ahead.

Variations
Try your favorite chocolate cake mix.

Replace pecans with unblanched almonds. Use whole almonds in the topping.

CAKE

1	pkg (18.25 oz/515 g]) white cake mix	1
1	pkg (4-serving size) vanilla instant pudding mix	1
4	eggs	4
1 1/3 cups	sour cream	325 mL
1/2 cup	vegetable oil	125 mL
1 1/2 cups	chopped pecans	375 mL

PECAN PRALINE TOPPING

1	egg white	1
1 tbsp	water	15 mL
1/2 cup	packed brown sugar	125 mL
1 1/2 cups	pecan halves	375 mL

CREAM CHEESE FROSTING

12 oz	cream cheese, softened	375 g
1/2 cup	butter, softened	125 mL
2 tsp	vanilla	10 mL
4 cups	confectioner's (icing) sugar, sifted	1 L

1. **Cake:** In a large mixer bowl, combine cake mix, pudding mix, eggs, sour cream and oil. Beat on medium speed for 2 minutes. Fold in pecans. Spread batter in prepared pans, dividing evenly. Bake for 30 to 35 minutes or until a tester inserted in the center comes out clean. Cool 10 minutes in pans on a wire rack, then remove and cool completely on rack.

2. *Pecan Praline Topping:* Preheat oven to 300°F (150°C). In a small bowl, beat egg white and water with a fork until foamy. Add brown sugar, mixing until sugar dissolves. Add pecans, tossing to coat nuts with sugar mixture. Spread on prepared baking sheet. Bake for 25 minutes, stirring occasionally until nuts are crisp and browned. Remove from oven. Stir to loosen nuts from sheet. Cool completely on sheet.

3. *Cream Cheese Frosting:* In a large mixer bowl, beat cream cheese, butter and vanilla until light and fluffy. Gradually add confectioner's sugar, beating until smooth.

4. *Assembly:* Place 1 cake top-side down on serving plate. Spread 1½ cups (375 mL) of the frosting over cake. Top with second cake layer, top-side up. Spread remaining frosting over top and sides of cake. Arrange Pecan Praline Topping over cake, mounding slightly in center. Refrigerate until serving. Store in the refrigerator.

Mocha Toffee Cake

Preheat oven to 350°F (180°C)
Three 9-inch (23 cm) round cake pans, greased and floured

SERVES 12 TO 16

With a layer of frosting covered by a whipped cream topping, this cake is definitely decadent — but one bite will convince you that it's worth every calorie.

Tips
Use cold strong coffee instead of the water and coffee powder.

Chill chocolate bars for easy crushing.

To save time when assembling the cake, prepare cake layers ahead and freeze. Defrost for 1 hour before assembly.

Variation
If you don't like the taste of coffee, you can omit it. Use water for the cake and replace the liqueur in the frosting with milk or cream.

CAKE

1	pkg (18.25 oz/515 g) devil's food cake mix	1
1 tbsp	instant coffee powder	15 mL
3	eggs	3
1 cup	water	250 mL
½ cup	sour cream	125 mL
⅓ cup	vegetable oil	75 mL

WHITE CHOCOLATE COFFEE FROSTING

½ cup	whipping (35%) cream	125 mL
4 oz	white chocolate, chopped	125 g
⅓ cup	coffee liqueur or cold strong coffee	75 mL
1 cup	butter, softened	250 mL
2 cups	confectioner's (icing) sugar, sifted	500 mL

WHIPPED CREAM TOPPING & GARNISH

2 cups	whipping (35%) cream	500 mL
3 tbsp	confectioner's (icing) sugar, sifted	45 mL
4	toffee chocolate bars (1.4 oz/40 g each), crushed	4

1. **Cake:** In a large mixer bowl, combine cake mix, coffee powder, eggs, water, sour cream and oil. Beat on medium speed for 2 minutes. Spread in prepared pans, dividing evenly. Bake for 20 to 25 minutes or until a tester inserted in the center comes out clean. Cool 10 minutes in pans on a wire rack, then remove and cool completely on rack.

2. *White Chocolate Coffee Frosting:* In a small saucepan, heat whipping cream and white chocolate on low heat, stirring until melted. Remove from heat. Stir in liqueur. Refrigerate about 45 minutes, until cool. In a large mixer bowl, beat butter and confectioner's sugar on medium speed until light and creamy. Gradually add chocolate mixture, beating until smooth.

3. *Whipped Cream Topping:* In a large mixer bowl, beat whipping cream and confectioner's sugar to stiff peaks.

4. *Assembly:* Place 1 cake, top-side down on serving plate. Spread with ¾ cup (175 mL) of White Chocolate Coffee Frosting. Repeat with remaining cake layers and frosting, ending with a cake layer, top-side up. Frost sides and top of cake with remaining White Chocolate Coffee Frosting. Chill about 30 minutes, until firm. Spread Whipped Cream Topping on sides and top of cake. Press crushed candy on sides and top of cake. Store in the refrigerator.

Chocolate Orange Marble Cake

Preheat oven to 350°F (180°C)
Two 9-inch (23 cm) round cake pans, greased and floured

SERVES 12 TO 16

Not only is this cake attractive, the combination of chocolate and orange liqueur is delicious.

Tips
Slices of orange gumdrops look nice on this cake and a simple drizzle of melted chocolate adds a finishing touch.

Remember to zest the orange before juicing.

Variation
Use a chocolate frosting for another great look and taste.

CAKE

1	pkg (18.25 oz/515 g) marble cake mix	1
3	eggs	3
2/3 cup	each orange juice and water	150 mL
1/3 cup	vegetable oil	75 mL
1 tbsp	grated orange zest	15 mL

ORANGE FROSTING

1/2 cup	butter, softened	125 mL
6 cups	confectioner's (icing) sugar, sifted	1.5 L
1/3 cup	whipping (35%) cream	75 mL
1/3 cup	orange juice	75 mL
1 tbsp	grated orange zest	15 mL

1. **Cake:** In a large mixer bowl, combine large cake mix envelope, eggs, orange juice, water and oil. Beat on medium speed for 2 minutes. Spoon 2 cups (500 mL) of the batter into a small bowl and stir in pouch of chocolate mix. Stir orange zest into white batter and divide evenly between prepared pans. Drop chocolate batter by spoonfuls randomly onto white batter. Run tip of knife through batters to create a marble effect. Bake for 30 to 35 minutes or until a tester inserted in the center comes out clean. Cool 10 minutes in pans on a wire rack, then remove and cool completely on rack.

2. **Orange Frosting:** In a large mixer bowl, beat butter on high speed until creamy. Add sugar alternately with cream and juice, beating until smooth. Stir in orange zest.

3. **Assembly:** Place 1 cake top-side down on a serving plate. Spread a generous amount, about 1 1/2 cups (375 mL) of frosting, over top. Place second cake top-side up over frosting. Frost top and sides of cake with remaining frosting. Decorate as desired.

Lemon Cream Torte

Preheat oven to 350°F (180°C)
Two 9-inch (23 cm) round cake pans, greased and floured

SERVES 12 TO 16

If you like lemon, you'll love this cake.

Tip
Since the filling thickens as it is left standing, set it aside for 5 minutes before adding the cream.

Use fresh lemon juice for the best flavour. Remember to zest the lemon before juicing.

Variation
For an extra hit of lemon, use a lemon cake mix.

CAKE

1	pkg (18.25 oz/515 g) white cake mix	1
3	eggs	3
1⅓ cups	water	325 mL
⅓ cup	vegetable oil	75 mL
1 tbsp	grated lemon zest	15 mL

FILLING

1	can (10 oz/300 mL) sweetened condensed milk	1
1 tbsp	grated lemon zest	15 mL
½ cup	lemon juice	125 mL
2 cups	whipping (35%) cream	500 mL
	Lemon slices, optional	

1. **Cake:** In a large mixer bowl, combine cake mix, eggs, water, oil and lemon zest. Beat on medium speed for 2 minutes. Spread batter in prepared pans, dividing evenly. Bake for 30 to 35 minutes or until a tester inserted in the center comes out clean. Cool 10 minutes in pans on a wire rack, then remove and cool completely on rack. With a sharp knife, cut each cake horizontally in half to make 4 layers.

2. **Filling:** In a small bowl, combine sweetened condensed milk, lemon zest and juice. Mix well. In a large mixer bowl, beat whipping cream to stiff peaks. Reserve 1 cup (250 mL) for garnish. Fold milk mixture into remaining whipped cream, gently but thoroughly.

3. **Assembly:** Place 1 cake layer, cut-side up on serving plate. Spread with one-quarter of filling. Repeat with second and third cake layers. Top with fourth cake layer, cut-side down. Spread remaining filling on top leaving a ½-inch (1 cm) border around edge. Pipe reserved cream around edge. Chill at least 2 hours before serving. Garnish with lemon slices, if desired. Store in the refrigerator.

49

Blueberry Lemon Cake

Preheat oven to 350°F (180°C)
Three 9-inch (23 cm) round cake pans, greased and floured

SERVES 12 TO 16

This cake is creamy, light and lemony — how can you go wrong?

Tip
If berries are moist, dust lightly with flour before adding them to the batter.

Variation
Try cranberries or raspberries in place of the blueberries.

CAKE

1	pkg (18.25 oz/515 g) lemon cake mix	1
1	pkg (4-serving size) vanilla instant pudding mix	1
4	eggs	4
¾ cup	sour cream	175 mL
¼ cup	vegetable oil	50 mL
2 cups	fresh blueberries	500 mL

LEMON CREAM CHEESE FROSTING

1 lb	cream cheese, softened	500 g
¾ cup	butter, softened	175 mL
4 cups	confectioner's (icing) sugar, sifted	1 L
1 tbsp	grated lemon zest	15 mL

1. **Cake:** In a large mixer bowl, combine cake mix, pudding mix, eggs, sour cream and oil. Beat on low speed for 1 minute to blend, then on medium speed for 2 minutes. Fold in blueberries, gently but thoroughly. Spread batter evenly in prepared pans. Bake for 25 to 30 minutes or until a tester inserted in the center comes out clean. Cool 10 minutes in pans on a wire rack, then remove and cool completely on rack.

2. **Lemon Cream Cheese Frosting:** In a large mixer bowl, beat cream cheese and butter until light and fluffy. Gradually add confectioner's sugar, beating until smooth. Stir in lemon zest.

3. **Assembly:** Place 1 cake top-side down on a serving plate. Spread about ¾ cup (175 mL) frosting on top. Repeat with second cake and frosting. Top with third cake layer top-side up. Spread remaining frosting on top and sides of cake. Store in the refrigerator.

Coconut Walnut Carrot Cake

Preheat oven to 350°F (180°C)
Two 9-inch (23 cm) round cake pans, greased and floured

SERVES 12 TO 16

Coconut adds a different texture and taste to a favorite cake. The layer cake presentation is a nice look.

Tips
Flaked rather than shredded coconut provides the best texture in most recipes.

Traditional cream cheese frosting goes well with this cake. Give it a boost by adding a garnish of toasted coconut.

Variation
Hazelnuts, almonds or pecans can replace walnuts.

1	pkg (18.25 oz/515 g) white cake mix	1
1	pkg (4-serving size) vanilla instant pudding mix	1
4	eggs	4
2½ cups	grated peeled carrots	625 mL
⅓ cup	vegetable oil	75 mL
¼ cup	water	50 mL
1 tsp	ground cinnamon	5 mL
1 tsp	ground ginger	5 mL
½ tsp	ground nutmeg	2 mL
⅔ cup	chopped walnuts	150 mL
⅔ cup	flaked coconut	150 mL

1. In a large mixer bowl, combine cake mix, pudding mix, eggs, carrots, oil, water, cinnamon, ginger and nutmeg. Beat on low speed for 1 minute to blend, then on medium speed for 2 minutes. Stir in walnuts and coconut. Spread batter in prepared pans, dividing evenly. Bake for 35 to 40 minutes or until a tester inserted in the center comes out clean. Cool 10 minutes in pans on a wire rack, then remove and cool completely on rack. Fill and frost cakes as desired.

51

Chocolate Strawberry Shortcake

Preheat oven to 350°F (180°C)
Two 9-inch (23 cm) round cake pans, greased and floured

SERVES 10 TO 12

You don't have to spend much time in the kitchen to get rave reviews for this dessert.

Tip
Dip tips of whole strawberries in chocolate for an exquisite finish. If time is critical, use two-thirds of the chocolate for the drizzle and leave strawberries plain.

Variation
A mixture of raspberries, blueberries and strawberries also works well in this recipe.

CAKE

1	pkg (18.25 oz/515 g) devil's food cake mix	1
2	eggs	2
1¼ cups	water	300 mL
⅓ cup	vegetable oil	75 mL

FILLING & TOPPING

3 oz	semi-sweet chocolate, chopped	90 g
1 tbsp	shortening	15 mL
2 tbsp	orange liqueur or orange juice	25 mL
2 cups	whipping (35%) cream	500 mL
¼ cup	confectioner's (icing) sugar, sifted	50 mL
3 cups	fresh strawberries	750 mL

1. **Cake:** In a large mixer bowl, combine cake mix, eggs, water and oil. Beat on medium speed for 2 minutes. Spread batter in prepared pans, dividing evenly. Bake according to package directions. Cool 10 minutes in pans on a wire rack, then remove and cool completely on rack. Freeze 1 cake for another use. With a long sharp knife, cut remaining cake horizontally in half.

2. **Filling & Topping:** In the top of a double boiler, over hot water, partially melt chocolate with shortening. (You can also do this in the microwave on medium power for 2 minutes.) Stir until smooth. Dip 7 strawberries in chocolate. Place on waxed paper and chill to set. Save remaining chocolate for the drizzle. Hull and cut remaining berries in half or thick slices. Brush each cake layer with 1 tbsp (15 mL) of the orange liqueur. In a large mixer bowl, beat whipping cream and confectioner's sugar to stiff peaks.

3. *Assembly:* Place 1 cake layer, cut-side up on serving plate. Spread half of whipped cream on top. Scatter sliced strawberries over cream. Place second cake layer cut-side down over berries. Top with remaining whipped cream. If necessary, heat reserved chocolate mixture again to soften. Drizzle over cream. Arrange dipped strawberries on top of cake. Chill until serving. Store leftover cake in the refrigerator.

Pineapple Orange Cake

Preheat oven to 350°F (180°C)
Two 9-inch (23 cm) round cake pans, greased and floured

SERVES 10 TO 12

The combination of orange and pineapple is both fresh and exotically tropical in this simple yet delicious cake.

Tip
Icing sugar, confectioner's sugar and powdered sugar are different names for the same thing. This type of sugar has been finely ground and cornstarch has been added. Since it tends to settle and can lump during storage, for easy blending, it should be sifted after measuring, before it is combined with other ingredients.

Variations
Try substituting pineapple or peach gelatin for the orange.

Fill and frost the cake with Orange Butter Frosting (see recipe, page 173) instead of the whipped cream.

CAKE

1	pkg (18.25 oz/515 g) white cake mix	1
1	pkg (3 oz/85 g) orange-flavoured gelatin dessert mix	1
4	eggs	4
1	can (14 oz/398 mL) crushed pineapple, including juice	1
1/3 cup	vegetable oil	75 mL
2	recipes Orange-Flavored Whipped Cream (see recipe, page 176) Orange slices, optional	2

1. **Cake:** In a large mixer bowl, combine cake mix, gelatin, eggs, pineapple (including juice) and oil. Beat on medium speed for 2 minutes. Spread batter in prepared pans, dividing evenly. Bake for 30 to 35 minutes or until a tester inserted in the center comes out clean. Cool 10 minutes in pans on a wire rack, then remove and cool completely on rack.

2. **Assembly:** Prepare Orange-Flavored Whipped Cream (doubling the recipe). Place 1 cake layer top-side down on a serving plate. Spread half of cream mixture on top. Place remaining cake layer top-side up over cream and cover with remaining cream. Decorate with orange slices, if desired. Chill until serving. Store leftover cake in the refrigerator.

Chocolate Fleck Banana Layer Cake

Preheat oven to 350°F (180°C)
Two 8-inch (20 cm) or 9-inch (23 cm) round cake pans, greased and floured

SERVES 10 TO 12

The riper the bananas, the better the flavor of this cake.

Tip
The hardest part of this recipe is grating the chocolate. I prefer to do it on a hand grater because it produces a coarser result, but the food processor is easier.

CAKE

1	pkg (18.25 oz/515 g) white cake mix	1
4	eggs	4
1⅔ cups	mashed ripe bananas (3 to 4 large bananas)	400 mL
⅓ cup	vegetable oil	75 mL
3 oz	semi-sweet chocolate, coarsely grated, divided	90 g

FROSTING

Banana Butter Frosting
(see recipe, page 179)

1. **Cake:** In a large mixer bowl, combine cake mix, eggs, mashed bananas and oil. Beat on medium speed for 2 minutes. Stir in two-thirds of the grated chocolate. Set remainder aside. Spread batter in prepared pans, dividing evenly. Bake for 30 to 35 minutes or until a tester inserted in the center comes out clean. Cool 10 minutes in pans on a wire rack, then remove and cool completely on rack.

2. **Frosting:** Prepare Banana Butter Frosting. Stir in reserved grated chocolate.

3. **Assembly:** Place 1 cake top-side down on a serving plate. Spread about ¾ cup (175 mL) frosting on top. Place remaining cake, top-side up over frosting. Cover sides and top of cake with remaining frosting. Chill until serving.

Chocolate Peanut Butter Cake

Preheat oven to 350°F (180°C)
Two 8-inch (20 cm) or 9-inch (23 cm) round cake pans, greased and floured

SERVES 10 TO 12

Peanut butter and chocolate are always a hit with kids young and old.

1	pkg (18.25 oz/515 g) devil's food cake mix	1
$1/2$ cup	creamy peanut butter	125 mL
3	eggs	3
$1^1/_3$ cups	water	325 mL
	Very Peanut Buttery Frosting (see recipe, page 179)	
	Decoration (optional)	
	Chocolate covered peanuts, chopped peanuts or halved chocolate peanut butter cups	

1. **Cake:** In a large mixer bowl, combine cake mix, peanut butter, eggs and water. Beat on medium speed for 2 minutes. Spread batter in prepared pans, dividing evenly. Bake 30 to 35 minutes or until a tester inserted in the center comes out clean. Cool 10 minutes in pans on a wire rack, then remove and cool completely on rack.

2. **Assembly:** Prepare Very Peanut Buttery Frosting. Place 1 cake top-side down on a serving plate. Spread a generous amount ($1^1/_2$ cups/375 mL) of frosting over top. Place second cake, top-side up over frosting. Frost top and sides of cake with remaining frosting. Decorate as desired.

Tips

Use creamy peanut butter for a creamy frosting or the crunchy variety if you like texture. Since the cake requires a smooth peanut butter, you can always add crunch with a sprinkling of chopped peanuts over the top and sides of the frosted cake.

Store peanuts in the freezer for maximum flavor retention.

Whether you use salted or unsalted nuts is a personal preference.

Variation

Use a chocolate frosting for a different look and taste.

Pineapple Banana Cake

Preheat oven to 350°F (180°C)
Two 9-inch (23 cm) round cake pans, greased and floured

SERVES 10 TO 12

This cake is very moist and full of flavor. It keeps well, too.

Tips
To ease the removal of cakes from a pan, grease the pan with shortening or cooking spray and dust with flour, shaking out the excess. Another alternative is to cut rounds of parchment paper to fit the bottom of the pan, which eliminates the need to grease and flour.

Dried banana slices make an attractive and crunchy garnish on this cake.

Variation
A plain butter frosting (see Basic Butter Frosting, page 173) with ⅓ cup (75 mL) well-drained crushed pineapple mixed in is also nice with this cake.

1	pkg (18.25 oz/515 g) white cake mix	1
3	eggs	3
1½ cups	mashed ripe bananas (3 to 4 large bananas)	375 mL
⅓ cup	vegetable oil	75 mL
½ cup	well-drained crushed pineapple	125 mL
	Pineapple Cream Cheese Frosting (see recipe, page 171)	

1. **Cake:** In a large mixer bowl, combine cake mix, eggs, bananas and oil. Beat on medium speed for 2 minutes. Stir in pineapple. Spread batter in prepared pans, dividing evenly. Bake for 35 to 40 minutes or until a tester inserted in the center comes out clean. Cool 10 minutes in pans on a wire rack, then remove and cool completely on rack.

2. **Assembly:** Prepare Pineapple Cream Cheese Frosting. Place 1 cake top-side down on serving plate. Spread a generous amount (1½ cups/375 mL) of frosting on top. Place second cake top-side up over frosting. Cover top and sides of cake with remaining frosting. Chill until serving to firm up frosting for neater slicing.

Chocolate Raspberry Torte

Preheat oven to 350°F (180°C)
Two 9-inch (23 cm) round cake pans, greased and floured

SERVES 10 TO 12

What could be more decadent than this chocolate cake, topped with chocolate and raspberry cream? And it's easy-to-make, as well.

Tips

For a Valentine's or a Mother's Day surprise, bake cakes in heart-shaped pans.

For a dynamite presentation, garnish with fresh raspberries and chocolate leaves.

Variations

Use a dark chocolate cake mix, such as German chocolate or fudge in place of devil's food.

Replace raspberries with strawberries.

CAKE

1	pkg (18.25 oz/515 g) devil's food cake mix	1
3	eggs	3
1 cup	sour cream	250 mL
¾ cup	water	175 mL
⅓ cup	vegetable oil	75 mL
1½ cups	miniature semi-sweet chocolate chips	325 mL

CHOCOLATE GANACHE

1 cup	semi-sweet chocolate chips	250 mL
½ cup	whipping (35%) cream	125 mL
1 tbsp	butter	15 mL
1 tbsp	raspberry or orange liqueur, optional	15 mL

RASPBERRY CREAM

1	pkg (10 oz/284 g) frozen raspberries in syrup, thawed	1
2 tbsp	granulated sugar	25 mL
2 tbsp	cornstarch	25 mL
½ cup	whipping (35%) cream	125 mL

1. **Cake:** In a large mixer bowl, combine cake mix, eggs, sour cream, water and oil. Beat on medium speed for 2 minutes. Stir in chocolate chips. Spread batter in prepared pans, dividing evenly. Bake for 35 to 40 minutes or until a tester inserted in the center comes out clean. Cool 10 minutes in pans on a wire rack, then remove and cool completely on rack. Wrap and freeze 1 layer for another use.

2. Chocolate Ganache: In a small saucepan, combine chocolate chips and whipping cream. Heat on low heat, stirring often until melted and smooth. Remove from heat. Add butter and liqueur, stirring until smooth. Refrigerate 1 to $1\frac{1}{2}$ hours, stirring occasionally until cold. Beat with wooden spoon or electric mixer on low speed until a thick creamy spreading consistency is reached.

3. Raspberry Cream: To remove seeds, place raspberries in a strainer over a small saucepan. Press with back of spoon. Discard seeds. Mix sugar and cornstarch. Add to raspberry juice stirring until smooth. Cook over medium heat, stirring constantly until mixture comes to a boil and is thickened. Boil for 1 minute. Transfer to a bowl and cover surface with plastic wrap. Chill for about 1 hour or until cold. In a large mixer bowl, beat cream to stiff peaks. Fold into raspberry mixture.

4. Assembly: Place cake top-side down on a serving plate. Spread with about $\frac{1}{3}$ cup (75 mL) of chocolate ganache. Cover sides of cake with about half of remaining ganache. Pipe remainder around the top and bottom edge of cake. Spread raspberry cream on top of cake inside the chocolate border. Chill until serving. Store leftover cake in refrigerator.

Chocolate Cake with Chocolate Raspberry Frosting

Preheat oven to 350°F (180°C)
Two 9-inch (23 cm) round cake pans, greased and floured

SERVES 10 TO 12

Fresh raspberries and chocolate are an unbeatable combination.

Tips
Fresh raspberries always have the most flavor and bright red color when in season. You can, however, often get excellent imported raspberries year round.

Serve cake at room temperature, about 1 hour after it is removed from the refrigerator, so the frosting is soft and creamy.

Variations
A mixture of raspberries and blackberries is nice.

Replace raspberry liqueur with orange liqueur or brandy.

CAKE

| 1 | pkg (18.25 oz/515 g) devil's food cake mix | 1 |

CHOCOLATE RASPBERRY FROSTING

1 lb	bittersweet chocolate, chopped	500 g
1⅓ cups	sour cream	325 mL
⅓ cup	seedless raspberry jam, stirred	75 mL
¼ cup	corn syrup	50 mL
2 tbsp	raspberry liqueur	25 mL
¼ cup	butter, softened	50 mL

FILLING & TOPPING

| ⅓ cup | seedless raspberry jam | 75 mL |
| 2 to 3 cups | fresh raspberries | 500 to 750 mL |

1. **Cake:** Prepare cake mix according to package directions. Spread batter in prepared pans, dividing evenly. Bake for 30 to 35 minutes or until a tester inserted in the center comes out clean. Cool 10 minutes in pans on a wire rack, then remove and cool completely on rack. With a long sharp knife, cut cakes horizontally in half to make 4 layers.

2. **Chocolate Raspberry Frosting:** In the top of a double boiler, over hot water, melt chocolate, stirring constantly until smooth. (You can also melt the chocolate in a microwave oven.) Pour into a large mixer bowl. Cool to room temperature. Add sour cream, jam, corn syrup and liqueur to chocolate. Beat on medium speed until light and fluffy, about 3 minutes. Beat in butter.

3. ***Assembly:*** Place 1 cake layer, cut-side up on a serving plate. Spread 2 tbsp (25 mL) jam on top. Spread about ¾ cup (175 mL) frosting over jam. Repeat layering twice more. Top with fourth cake layer, cut-side down. Spread remaining frosting over top and sides of cake. Arrange fresh raspberries on top of cake. Chill. Remove cake from refrigerator about 1 hour before serving. Store leftover cake in refrigerator.

Piña Colada Cake

Preheat oven to 350°F (180°C)
Two 8-inch (20 cm) or 9-inch (23 cm) round cake pans, greased and floured

SERVES 10 TO 12

The combination of flavours — pineapple, coconut and rum — immortalized in the famous cocktail is equally delicious in a cake.

Tips

All the parts can be prepared up to 3 days ahead and the cake can be assembled the day before.

Light rum will not discolor the cake but if you only have amber, the taste will still be awesome!

Shaved coconut is attractive and makes a nice finish for cakes. It's available in South Asian grocery stores.

CAKE

1	pkg (18.25 oz/515 g) white cake mix	1

PINEAPPLE FILLING

1	can (19 oz/398 mL) crushed pineapple, including juice	1
2 tbsp	granulated sugar	25 mL
2 tbsp	cornstarch	25 mL
1 tsp	lemon juice	5 mL

RUM SYRUP

2/3 cup	water	150 mL
1/3 cup	granulated sugar	75 mL
3 tbsp	rum	45 mL

COCONUT BUTTERCREAM

1 cup	butter, softened	250 mL
3 1/2 cups	confectioner's (icing) sugar, sifted	825 mL
3 to 4 tbsp	light (10%) cream	45 to 60 mL
1 tsp	coconut extract	5 mL

GARNISH

3 1/2 cups	shaved coconut	825 mL

1. **Cake:** Prepare cake mix as directed on package. Spread batter in prepared pans, dividing evenly. Bake for 30 to 35 minutes or until a tester inserted in the center comes out clean. Cool 10 minutes in pans on a wire rack, then remove and cool completely on rack. With a long sharp knife, but cakes horizontally in half to make 4 layers.

Tips
Lightly-toasted coconut has a sweeter flavor and a crunchy rather than chewy texture.

The flavor of coconut extract intensifies if it's left to stand. Keep this in mind if you're preparing the cake ahead.

Variations
Replace the shaved coconut with flaked.

Add 1 tsp (5 mL) coconut extract to the cake batter for a stronger coconut taste.

2. *Pineapple Filling:* In a saucepan, combine pineapple with juice, sugar, cornstarch and lemon juice. Cook, stirring constantly over medium heat until mixture comes to a boil, then simmer 3 minutes. Cool completely.

3. *Rum Syrup:* In a small saucepan, combine water and sugar. Bring to a boil, stirring until sugar is dissolved. Remove from heat. Stir in rum. Cool completely.

4. *Coconut Buttercream:* In a large mixer bowl, beat butter and half of confectioner's sugar until light and creamy. Add cream and coconut extract. Gradually add remaining confectioner's sugar, beating until smooth. Add enough cream to make a soft spreading consistency.

5. *Assembly:* Place 1 cake layer, cut-side up on a serving plate. Brush top with some rum syrup. Spread half of pineapple filling on top. Top with another cake layer. Brush with syrup and spread ¾ cup (175 mL) buttercream on top. Top with third cake layer. Brush with syrup and spread remaining pineapple over it. Place fourth cake layer on top, cut-side down. Brush with remaining syrup. Frost top and sides with remaining buttercream. Cover with coconut, pressing into buttercream lightly. Chill until serving. Store leftover cake in the refrigerator.

Ice Cream Loaf Cake

Preheat oven to 350°F (180°C)
Two 9- by 5-inch (1.5 L) loaf pans, greased and floured

SERVES 8

Here's a great dessert that you can keep in your freezer for unexpected company.

Tips
To soften, let ice cream sit at room temperature about 15 minutes. This makes it easier to shape.

Ice cream is more easily cut from the rectangular blocks than it is spooned from the tubs. Freeze the ice cream loaf until firm, then wrap in foil for longer storage.

Variation
Vary the flavor of ice cream to suit your taste.

CAKE

1	pkg (18.25 oz/515 g) white cake mix	1
1	pkg (4-serving size) vanilla instant pudding mix	1
4	eggs	4
½ cup	sour cream	125 mL
¼ cup	vegetable oil	50 mL

FILLING

2 cups	each chocolate and strawberry ice cream, softened	500 mL

FROSTING

2 cups	whipping (35%) cream	500 mL
¼ cup	confectioner's (icing) sugar, sifted	50 mL
	Shaved chocolate or toasted coconut to garnish, optional	

1. **Cake:** In a large mixer bowl, combine cake mix, pudding mix, eggs, sour cream and oil. Beat on medium speed for 2 minutes. Spread batter in prepared pans, dividing evenly. Bake for 40 to 45 minutes or until a tester inserted in the center comes out clean. Cool 20 minutes in pan on a wire rack then remove and cool completely on rack. Freeze 1 loaf cake for later use. With long sharp knife, cut remaining cake horizontally into 3 layers.

2. **Filling:** Place bottom cake layer on serving platter. Spread chocolate ice cream evenly on top. Spread middle cake layer with strawberry ice cream and place on top of bottom layer. Top with third cake layer. Freeze until firm.

3. **Frosting:** In a large mixer bowl, beat whipping cream and confectioner's sugar until stiff peaks form. Spread on sides and top of loaf. Garnish top, if desired. Freeze until firm. Remove from freezer 10 minutes before serving.

Lemon Poppy Seed Ring *(page 71)* ▶
Overleaf: Triple Raspberry Treat *(page 40)*

Cranberry Orange Cake

Preheat oven to 350°F (180°C)
Two 9-inch (23 cm) round cake pans, greased and floured

SERVES 12 TO 16

Here's a cake with flavor that dazzles.

Tips
My first choice for juice is freshly squeezed, followed by commercially-prepared juice with pulp.

After removing the zest, warm oranges slightly in the microwave to get the most juice.

Sliced almonds are a nice garnish on this cake.

Variation
Replace whipped topping with 2 cups (500 mL) whipping (35%) cream slightly sweetened and beaten to stiff peaks.

CAKE

1	pkg (18.25 oz/515 g) white cake mix	1
3	eggs	3
1 tbsp	grated orange zest	15 mL
1 1/3 cups	orange juice	325 mL
1/3 cup	vegetable oil	75 mL

FROSTING

1	can (14 oz/398 mL) whole berry instant cranberry sauce	1
1	pkg (4-serving size) vanilla pudding mix	1
1 tbsp	grated orange zest	15 mL
1/2 cup	orange juice	125 mL
4 cups	frozen whipped topping, thawed	1 L

1. **Cake:** In a large mixer bowl, combine cake mix, eggs, orange zest and juice and oil. Beat on medium speed for 2 minutes. Spread batter in prepared pans, dividing evenly. Bake for 25 to 30 minutes or until a tester inserted in the center comes out clean. Cool 10 minutes in pans on a wire rack, then remove and cool completely on rack. With a long sharp knife, cut cakes horizontally in half to make 4 layers.

2. **Frosting:** In a bowl, combine cranberry sauce, pudding mix, orange zest and juice. Mix well. Let stand 10 minutes to thicken. Fold in whipped topping, gently but thoroughly.

3. **Assembly:** Place 1 cake layer, cut-side up on a serving plate. Spread with 3/4 cup (175 mL) of the frosting. Repeat with remaining cake layers and frosting, ending with a cake layer, cut-side down. Spread frosting on sides and top of cake. Chill until serving. Store leftover cake in the refrigerator.

◀ *Cranberry Almond Coffee Cake (page 92)*

Spice Cake with Blackberries

Preheat oven to 350°F (180°C)
Three 8-inch (20 cm) or 9-inch (23 cm) round cake pans, greased and floured

SERVES 10 TO 12

Fresh blackberries and a creamy frosting add a touch of sophistication to spice cake.

Tips
Prepare cake the day before, for convenience. Leave the final berry garnish until you're ready to serve.

If you can't find a spice cake mix, add 2 tsp (10 mL) ground cinnamon and ½ tsp (2 mL) each ground nutmeg and cloves to a white cake mix.

Variation
Raspberries are a tasty and attractive alternative to blackberries.

CAKE

1	pkg (18.25 oz/515 g) spice cake mix	1

FILLING

1½ cups	fresh blackberries	375 mL
¼ cup	granulated sugar	50 mL

FROSTING

1½	recipes Basic Cream Cheese Frosting (see recipe, page 171)	1½

GARNISH

1 cup	fresh blackberries	250 mL

1. Prepare cake mix according to package directions. Spread batter in prepared pans, dividing evenly. Bake for 20 to 25 minutes or until a tester inserted in the center comes out clean. Cool 10 minutes in pans on a wire rack, then remove and cool completely on rack.

2. *Filling:* Mash berries slightly with fork. Mix with sugar. Let stand about 30 minutes or until juices are released.

3. *Assembly:* Prepare Basic Cream Cheese Frosting as directed. Place 1 cake top-side down on a serving plate. Spread with 1 cup (250 mL) of frosting. Spread half of filling over frosting leaving a ½-inch (1 cm) plain border around edge. Repeat with second cake. Top with third cake, top-side up. Spread remaining frosting over top and sides of cake. Garnish with fresh blackberries. Chill until serving. Store leftover cake in the refrigerator.

Tube & Bundt Cakes

Butterscotch Swirl

Preheat oven to 350°F (180°C)
10-inch (4 L) tube pan, greased and floured

SERVES 12 TO 16

Here's a treat for those who prefer the flavor of butterscotch to chocolate.

Tips

Dark brown and golden brown sugar are interchangeable. The dark has a stronger flavor while golden has a more appealing color.

To ease cleanup when using a glaze, which unlike frosting tends to drip, set the wire rack over waxed paper.

CAKE

1	pkg (4-serving size) butterscotch instant pudding mix, divided	1
1	pkg (18.25 oz/515 g) white cake mix	1
2	eggs	2
1 1/3 cups	water	325 mL
1/4 cup	butter, softened	50 mL
1/2 cup	packed brown sugar	125 mL
2 tbsp	all-purpose flour	25 mL

GLAZE

1/4 cup	butter	50 mL
3 tbsp	reserved butterscotch instant pudding mix (see Step 1)	45 mL
2 tbsp	corn syrup	25 mL
2 tbsp	milk	25 mL
1 cup	confectioner's (icing) sugar, sifted	250 mL

1. **Cake:** Reserve 3 tbsp (45 mL) of the pudding mix for a glaze. In a large mixer bowl, combine remaining pudding mix, cake mix, eggs, water and butter. Beat on medium speed for 2 minutes. Reserve 1 cup (250 mL) of the batter. Spread remaining batter evenly in prepared pan. Add brown sugar and flour to reserved batter. Mix well. Spoon over batter in pan. Run tip of knife through batters to create a marble effect. Bake for 40 to 50 minutes or until a tester inserted in the center comes out clean. Cool 25 minutes in pan on a wire rack, then remove from pan and place on rack set over waxed paper.

2. **Glaze:** In a small saucepan, over low heat, stir butter, reserved pudding mix, corn syrup and milk until butter is melted and mixture is smooth. Remove from heat. Stir in confectioner's sugar. Quickly spoon warm glaze over warm cake. Let glaze set before cutting cake.

Double Chocolate Coconut Rum Cake

Preheat oven to 350°F (180°C)
10-inch (3 L) Bundt pan or (4 L) tube pan, greased and floured

SERVES 12 TO 16

Chock-full of ingredients, this rich and delicious cake is a great treat after a light meal.

Tips
If you're feeling adventurous, try using shaved coconut, which is usually sold in South Asian grocery stores, in this recipe. It has a different texture than flaked coconut. A light toasting looks attractive on the white frosting.

The soft glaze will melt slightly when applied to the warm cake. The waxed paper will catch any drips.

CAKE

1	pkg (18.25 oz/515 g) devil's food cake mix	1
1	pkg (4-serving size) chocolate instant pudding mix	1
4	eggs	4
1 cup	sour cream	250 mL
2/3 cup	whipping (35%) cream	150 mL
1/2 cup	vegetable oil	125 mL
3 tbsp	water	45 mL
3 tbsp	rum	45 mL
1 1/2 cups	white chocolate chips	375 mL
1 cup	flaked coconut	250 mL

GLAZE

1 2/3 cups	confectioner's (icing) sugar	400 mL
2 tbsp	butter, softened	25 mL
2 tbsp	milk	25 mL
1 tbsp	rum (approx.)	15 mL
	Coconut to garnish, optional	

1. **Cake:** In a large mixer bowl, combine cake mix, pudding mix, eggs, sour cream, whipping cream, oil, water and rum. Beat on low speed for 1 minute to blend, then on medium speed for 2 minutes. Stir in white chocolate chips and coconut. Spread batter evenly in prepared pan. Bake for 50 to 55 minutes or until a tester inserted in the center comes out clean. Cool 20 minutes in pan on a wire rack, then place on rack set over waxed paper.

2. **Glaze:** In a mixer bowl, combine confectioner's sugar, butter and milk. Beat on low speed, adding enough rum to make a smooth spreadable consistency. Spread on top and sides of warm cake. Sprinkle coconut over glaze, if desired. Cool completely before cutting cake.

69

Chocolate Cranberry Ring

Preheat oven to 350°F (180°C)
10-inch (4 L) tube pan, greased and floured

SERVES 12 TO 16

Here's a festive cake you can enjoy year round.

Tips
If using frozen cranberries, thaw and pat dry before folding into the batter.

The citrus glaze keeps the cake moist.

Variations
For an interesting color, use unblanched almonds.

Omit the glaze and dust with confectioner's sugar, just before serving.

Replace cranberries with blueberries.

CAKE

1	pkg (18.25 oz/515 g) white cake mix	1
1	pkg (4-serving size) vanilla instant pudding mix	1
4	eggs	4
1⅓ cups	sour cream	325 mL
½ cup	vegetable oil	125 mL
½ tsp	ground cinnamon	2 mL
1 cup	fresh cranberries or frozen, thawed	250 mL
1 cup	semi-sweet chocolate chips	250 mL
½ cup	sliced almonds	125 mL

GLAZE

¾ cup	granulated sugar	175 mL
3 tbsp	orange liqueur or juice	45 mL
3 tbsp	lemon juice	45 mL

1. **Cake:** In a large mixer bowl, combine cake mix, pudding mix, eggs, sour cream, oil and cinnamon. Beat on medium speed for 2 minutes. Fold in cranberries, chocolate chips and almonds. Spread batter evenly in prepared pan. Bake for 45 to 55 minutes or until a tester inserted in the center comes out clean. Cool 20 minutes in pan on a wire rack, then remove from pan and place on rack set over waxed paper.

2. **Glaze:** In a small saucepan, combine sugar, liqueur and lemon juice. Bring to a boil and simmer for 1 minute, until sugar is dissolved. Poke holes over surface of warm cake with fork or toothpick. Brush warm glaze over the top and sides of warm cake. Repeat until all the glaze is used up. Cool completely before cutting cake.

Lemon Poppy Seed Ring

Preheat oven to 350°F (180°C)
10-inch (4 L) tube pan, greased and floured

SERVES 12 TO 16

The lemon glaze soaks into the warm cake, making it moist and extra lemony.

Tips

Mix glaze ingredients ahead. If necessary, heat gently to dissolve sugar.

You can always use sour cream in place of yogurt in cake baking.

Freshly-squeezed lemon juice has the best flavor. Use it whenever possible.

Variation

Although we love the poppy seed crunch, this cake is also nice plain. It also works well with ½ cup (125 mL) finely chopped almonds instead of the poppy seeds.

CAKE

1	pkg (18.25 oz/515 g) lemon cake mix	1
1	pkg (4-serving size) vanilla instant pudding mix	1
4	eggs	4
1 cup	lemon or plain yogurt	250 mL
⅓ cup	vegetable oil	75 mL
¼ cup	poppy seeds	50 mL
2 tsp	grated lemon zest	10 mL

LEMON GLAZE

¾ cup	granulated sugar	175 mL
⅓ cup	lemon juice	75 mL

1. **Cake:** In a large mixer bowl, combine cake mix, pudding mix, eggs, yogurt, oil, poppy seeds and lemon zest. Beat on medium speed for 2 minutes. Spread batter evenly in prepared pan. Bake for 50 to 60 minutes or until a tester inserted in the center comes out clean. Cool 20 minutes in pan on a wire rack then remove from pan and place on rack set over waxed paper.

2. **Glaze:** In a small saucepan, over low heat combine sugar and lemon juice, stirring until sugar is dissolved. Poke holes over the surface of warm cake with a fork or a toothpick. Brush glaze over cake, letting it soak in. Cool completely before cutting cake.

Chocolate Zucchini Cake

Preheat oven to 350°F (180°C)
10-inch (4 L) tube pan, greased and floured

SERVES 12 TO 16

Moist, with lots of rich chocolate flavor, this cake is delicious with or without frosting. For a special treat, top with Chocolate Cream Cheese Frosting (see recipe, page 178) or a Chocolate Butter Frosting (see recipe, page 173).

Tip
When baking cakes, don't use grated zucchini that has been frozen. It is too wet for the batter and will result in soggy, dense cakes.

Variation
Omit chocolate chips or replace with additional chopped nuts.

1	pkg (18.25 oz/515 g) devil's food cake mix	1
3	eggs	3
¾ cup	water	175 mL
⅓ cup	vegetable oil	75 mL
½ tsp	ground cinnamon	2 mL
1½ cups	grated zucchini	375 mL
1 cup	semi-sweet chocolate chips	250 mL
½ cup	chopped nuts	125 mL

1. In a large mixer bowl, combine cake mix, eggs, water, oil and cinnamon. Beat on low speed for 1 minute to blend, then on medium speed for 2 minutes. Stir in zucchini, chocolate chips and nuts. Mix well. Spread batter evenly in prepared pan. Bake for 50 to 60 minutes or until a tester inserted in the center comes out clean. Cool 25 minutes in pan on a wire rack then remove from pan and cool completely on rack. Frost as desired.

Milk Chocolate Fleck Cake

Preheat oven to 350°F (180°C)
10-inch (3 L) Bundt pan, greased and floured

SERVES 12 TO 16

This tender moist cake has a very appealing mild chocolate taste. It makes a delicious coffee-time treat.

Tips
Grate chocolate in a food processor, for convenience. If using a hand grater, buy a chocolate bar that is slightly bigger than the quantity required to avoid scraping your knuckles.

If you are glazing this cake, let it cool completely first.

Finish with a drizzle of chocolate or a dusting of confectioner's sugar.

Variation
Use bittersweet chocolate, if you prefer a stronger chocolate taste.

CAKE

1	pkg (18.25 oz/515 g) white cake mix	1
1	pkg (4 serving size) vanilla instant pudding mix	1
4	eggs	4
1 cup	sour cream	250 mL
1/2 cup	vegetable oil	125 mL
7 oz	milk chocolate, coarsely grated	210 g

GLAZE, OPTIONAL

2 oz	milk chocolate, melted	60 g
1 tsp	vegetable oil	5 mL

1. **Cake:** In a large mixer bowl, combine cake mix, pudding mix, eggs, sour cream and oil. Beat on medium speed for 2 minutes. Stir in chocolate, gently but thoroughly. Spread batter evenly in prepared pan. Bake for 50 to 60 minutes or until a tester inserted in the center comes out clean. Cool 25 minutes in pan on a wire rack then remove from pan and place on rack. Enjoy warm or cool completely and glaze or sprinkle with confectioner's sugar.

2. **Glaze:** Stir oil into melted chocolate. Drizzle over cake. Chill to set chocolate.

73

Chocolate Cream Filled Bundt Cake

Preheat oven to 350°F (180°C)
10-inch (3 L) Bundt pan, greased and floured

SERVES 12 TO 16

The combination of dark chocolate cake drizzled with a bright white glaze and filled with a creamy white center is more than visually stunning. It's also delicious.

Tip
You can bake this cake, then freeze it before adding the finish. When ready to serve, thaw and drizzle with glaze or dust with confectioner's sugar.

Variation
For a dark chocolate color and richer flavor, use a chocolate fudge cake mix.

FILLING

8 oz	cream cheese, softened	250 g
¼ cup	granulated sugar	50 mL
1	egg	1
1 tsp	vanilla	5 mL

CAKE

1	pkg (18.25 oz/5.5 g) devil's food cake mix	1

GLAZE

1 cup	confectioner's (icing) sugar, sifted	250 mL
¼ tsp	vanilla	1 mL
1 to 2 tbsp	water or milk	15 to 25 mL

1. **Filling:** In a small mixer bowl, beat cream cheese and sugar on low speed until blended. Add egg and vanilla, beating until smooth, about 2 minutes. Set aside.

2. **Cake:** Prepare cake mix according to package directions. Pour 3 cups (750 mL) of the batter into prepared pan. Spoon filling over batter without touching sides of pan. Cover with remaining batter. Bake for 50 to 60 minutes or until a tester inserted into cake (avoiding filling) comes out clean. Cool for 30 minutes in pan on a wire rack, then remove from pan and cool completely on rack set over waxed paper.

3. **Glaze:** In a small bowl, combine confectioner's sugar and vanilla. Stir in enough water to make a smooth drizzling consistency. Drizzle over cake.

Fuzzy Navel Cake

Preheat oven to 350°F (180°C)
10-inch (3 L) Bundt pan, greased and floured

SERVES 12 TO 16

Here's a version of a fuzzy navel, a cocktail that combines peach schnapps and orange juice. It lets you have your drink and eat it, too.

Tips
Use shortening or cooking spray to grease cake pans. With oil and butter, the cakes tend to stick and burn.

Place cake over waxed paper to catch the drips when glazing.

Variation
Orange juice can replace orange liqueur, if desired.

CAKE

1	pkg (18.25 oz/515 g) white cake mix	1
1	pkg (3 oz/85 g) peach-flavored gelatin dessert mix	1
4	eggs	4
¾ cup	orange liqueur	175 mL
1 tbsp	grated orange zest	15 mL
½ cup	orange juice	125 mL
½ cup	vegetable oil	125 mL

GLAZE, OPTIONAL

1 cup	confectioner's (icing) sugar, sifted	250 mL
¼ cup	orange juice	50 mL
2 tbsp	orange liqueur	25 mL

1. *Cake:* In a large mixer bowl, combine cake mix, gelatin mix, eggs, liqueur, orange zest and juice and oil. Beat on medium speed for 2 minutes. Spread batter evenly in prepared pan. Bake for 45 to 55 minutes or until a tester inserted in the center comes out clean. Cool 20 minutes in pan on a wire rack, then remove from pan and invert on rack over waxed paper.

2. *Glaze:* In a bowl, combine confectioner's sugar, orange juice and liqueur, mixing until smooth. Poke holes over surface of warm cake with fork or toothpick. Brush glaze over cake, letting it soak in. Cool completely before cutting cake.

Lime Daiquiri Cake

Preheat oven to 350°F (180°C)
10-inch (3 L) Bundt or (4 L) tube pan, greased and floured

SERVES 12 TO 16

This cake is a delicious excuse to make Lime Cream, which is one of my favorite toppings.

Tips
One medium lime will yield about 2 tbsp (25 mL) juice and 1 tsp (5 mL) grated zest. To get the maximum amount of juice, squeeze the lime when it is at room temperature or even slightly warm.

Use the Lime Cream topping as a dip for fresh strawberries and cherries. It can be prepared a day ahead.

Variations
Use sweetened whipped cream as the topping, if desired.

CAKE

1	pkg (18.25 oz/515 g) white cake mix	1
3	eggs	3
⅔ cup	water	150 mL
⅓ cup	rum	75 mL
⅓ cup	vegetable oil	75 mL
1 tbsp	grated lime zest	15 mL
¼ cup	lime juice	50 mL
1 to 3	drops green food coloring, optional	1 to 3

GLAZE

½ cup	granulated sugar	125 mL
⅓ cup	lime juice	75 mL
¼ cup	rum	50 mL

LIME CREAM, OPTIONAL

½ cup	granulated sugar	125 mL
1	egg, beaten	1
1½ tsp	grated lime zest	7 mL
3 tbsp	lime juice	45 mL
2 tbsp	butter, softened	25 mL
1 cup	whipping (35%) cream	250 mL

1. **Cake:** In a large mixer bowl, combine cake mix, eggs, water, rum, oil, lime zest and juice. Beat on medium speed for 2 minutes. Stir in coloring, if desired. Spread batter evenly in prepared pan. Bake for 45 to 55 minutes or until a tester inserted in the center comes out clean. Cool for 20 minutes in pan on a wire rack, then invert onto rack over waxed paper.

2. *Glaze:* In a saucepan, over medium heat, combine sugar, lime juice and rum. Cook, stirring, just until sugar dissolves. Poke holes in warm cake with fork or toothpick. Brush glaze over cake letting it soak in. Cool completely. Serve with Lime Cream or whipped cream.

3. *Lime Cream:* In a small saucepan, combine sugar, egg, lime zest and juice. Cook, stirring constantly over medium heat, until thickened. Add butter, stirring until melted. Cool thoroughly. In a mixer bowl, on high speed beat cream to stiff peaks. Fold into lime mixture. Serve a dollop of Lime Cream on top of glazed cake.

Cranberry White Chocolate Orange Cake

Preheat oven to 350°F (180°C)
10-inch (4 L) tube pan, greased and floured

SERVES 12 TO 16

Don't limit this wonderful cake to cranberry season. Keep a bag of frozen berries on hand and enjoy them year round.

Tip
If using frozen cranberries, thaw and pat dry before folding into batter.

Variation
Replace cranberries with blueberries.

CAKE

1	pkg (18.25 oz/515 g) white cake mix	1
1	pkg (4-serving size) vanilla instant pudding mix	1
4	eggs	4
1⅓ cups	sour cream	325 mL
½ cup	vegetable oil	125 mL
1 tbsp	grated orange zest	15 mL
1 cup	cranberries, thawed if frozen	250 mL
4 oz	white chocolate, chopped	125 g

GLAZE

3 oz	white chocolate, chopped	90 g
2 tbsp	orange juice	25 mL

1. **Cake:** In a large mixer bowl, combine cake mix, pudding mix, eggs, sour cream, oil and orange zest. Beat on medium speed for 2 minutes. Fold in cranberries and white chocolate. Spread batter in prepared pan. Bake for 60 to 65 minutes or until a tester inserted in the center comes out clean. Cool 25 minutes in pans on a wire rack, then remove from pan and cool completely on rack set over waxed paper.

2. **Glaze:** In a saucepan over low heat or in microwave on medium for 1½ minutes, melt white chocolate and orange juice. Stir until smooth. Drizzle over cooled cake. Let chocolate set before cutting cake.

Double Chocolate Delight

Preheat oven to 350°F (180°C)
10-inch (3 L) Bundt pan, greased and floured

SERVES 12 TO 16

This delicious cake is very rich, very moist and very chocolatey. It may not last long but if it does, it keeps very well.

Tips
Always sift cocoa before using. It clumps during storage and the lumps don't come out, even during beating.

If you really want to overdose on chocolate, a chocolate drizzle (see page 15) makes a nice finish.

Variation
Replace semi-sweet chips with milk chocolate chips.

1	pkg (18.25 oz/515 g) white cake mix	1
1/3 cup	granulated sugar	75 mL
1/3 cup	unsweetened cocoa powder, sifted	75 mL
4	eggs	4
1 cup	sour cream	250 mL
2/3 cup	vegetable oil	150 mL
1 1/2 cups	miniature semi-sweet chocolate chips	375 mL

1. **Cake:** In a large mixer bowl, combine cake mix, sugar, cocoa, eggs, sour cream and oil. Beat on low speed for 1 minute to blend, then on medium speed for 2 minutes. Stir in chocolate chips. Spread batter evenly in prepared pan. Bake for 50 to 60 minutes or until a tester inserted in the center comes out clean. Cool 25 minutes in pan on a wire rack, then remove from pan and cool completely on rack.

Sherry Cake

Preheat oven to 350°F (180°C)
10-inch (4 L) tube pan, greased and floured

SERVES 12 TO 16

This traditional Portuguese cake is perfect to serve with a cup of coffee or with ice cream for a special dessert.

Tips

You can't go wrong with a bottle of sherry in your cupboard. It's nice to brush on fruitcake and to use as an ingredient in other cakes such as this.

This may seem like a lot of sherry, but the flavor is pleasantly mellow and not overpowering.

Variation

Try making this with a yellow cake mix.

CAKE

1	pkg (18.25 oz/515 g) white cake mix	1
1	pkg (4-serving size) vanilla instant pudding mix	1
4	eggs	4
¾ cup	cream sherry	175 mL
½ cup	vegetable oil	125 mL
¼ cup	butter, melted	50 mL
2 tsp	ground nutmeg	10 mL
¼ cup	granulated sugar	50 mL
1 tsp	ground cinnamon	5 mL

GLAZE

1 cup	confectioner's (icing) sugar, sifted	250 mL
2 tbsp	milk	25 mL
½ tsp	vanilla	2 mL

1. **Cake:** In a large mixer bowl, combine cake mix, pudding mix, eggs, sherry, oil, melted butter and nutmeg. Beat on medium speed for 2 minutes. In a separate bowl, combine sugar and cinnamon. Spread ⅓ of batter in prepared pan. Sprinkle ½ of sugar mixture on top. Add another ⅓ of batter and remaining sugar mixture. Cover with remaining batter. Bake for 45 to 50 minutes or until a tester inserted in the center comes out clean. Cool 25 minutes in pan on a wire rack then remove from pan and cool completely on rack set over waxed paper.

2. **Glaze:** In a bowl, combine confectioner's sugar, milk and vanilla, mixing until smooth. Drizzle over cooled cake. Let glaze set before cutting cake.

Decadent Chocolate Almond Cake

Preheat oven to 350°F (180°C)
10-inch (4 L) tube pan, greased and lined with parchment paper

SERVES 12 TO 16

Easy to make and loaded with chocolate — what could be better than this delicious, moist cake?

Tips
Chocolate bars tend to stick at the point where they come in contact with a pan. To avoid problems when removing the cake, line the bottom and sides of the pan with parchment paper.

For a grand finale, serve this cake with a dollop of whipped cream flavoured with amaretto.

Use blanched or unblanched almonds, as you prefer.

Variation
Replace almonds with hazelnuts.

CAKE

1	pkg (18.25 oz/515 g) devil's food cake mix, divided	1
4	toffee-crunch chocolate bars (each 1.4 oz/39 g), chopped	4
½ cup	chopped almonds	125 mL
1	pkg (4-serving size) chocolate instant pudding mix	1
4	eggs	4
1 cup	sour cream	250 mL
¼ cup	water	50 mL
¼ cup	almond liqueur	50 mL

GLAZE

3 tbsp	butter	45 mL
¼ cup	almond liqueur	50 mL
1 tbsp	granulated sugar	15 mL

1. **Cake:** In a small bowl, sprinkle 2 tbsp (30 mL) of the cake mix over chocolate bars and almonds. Toss to thoroughly coat. Set aside. In a large mixer bowl, combine remaining cake mix, pudding mix, eggs, sour cream, water and liqueur. Beat on medium speed for 2 minutes. Stir in chocolate bar mixture. Mix well. Spread batter evenly in prepared pan. Bake for 50 to 60 minutes or until a tester inserted in the center comes out clean. Cool 20 minutes in pan on a wire rack, then remove from pan and place on rack set over waxed paper.

2. **Glaze:** In a small saucepan, combine butter, liqueur and sugar. Bring to a boil, then simmer 1 minute, stirring, until sugar is dissolved and glaze is slightly thickened. Brush glaze over warm cake. Cool completely.

Chocolate Coffee Bundt Cake

Preheat oven to 350°F (180°C)
10-inch (3 L) Bundt pan, greased and floured

SERVES 12 TO 16

The unique buttery, sugary coffee glaze does more than keep this cake moist. It also makes it especially delicious.

Tips

Liqueurs can often be replaced with a similar-flavor non-alcoholic liquid in recipes. For example, in this cake you can use strong coffee for the coffee liqueur, if you prefer. Add to saucepan along with the other ingredients.

If desired, dust this cake with confectioner's sugar just before serving.

Variations

Replace coffee liqueur with orange. Omit cinnamon and add 1 tbsp (15 mL) grated orange zest to the batter.

GLAZE

1 cup	granulated sugar	250 mL
½ cup	butter	125 mL
½ cup	prepared black coffee	125 mL
¼ cup	coffee liqueur	50 mL

CAKE

1	pkg (18.25 oz/515 g) devil's food cake mix	1
1	pkg (4-serving size) chocolate instant pudding mix	1
4	eggs	4
½ cup	water	125 mL
¼ cup	coffee liqueur	50 mL
1 tsp	ground cinnamon	5 mL
1 cup	miniature semi-sweet chocolate chips	250 mL

1. **Glaze:** In a small saucepan, combine sugar, butter and coffee. Bring to a boil over medium heat, stirring to dissolve sugar, then boil 3 minutes. Remove from heat. Stir in liqueur. Let cool while preparing cake.

2. **Cake:** In a large mixer bowl, combine cake mix, pudding mix, eggs, water, liqueur and cinnamon. Beat on medium speed for 2 minutes. Stir in chocolate chips. Spread batter evenly in prepared pan. Bake for 50 to 55 minutes or until a tester inserted in the center comes out clean. Cool 20 minutes in pan on a wire rack, then remove from pan and cool completely on rack set over waxed paper.

3. Poke holes over surface of warm cake with fork or toothpick. Brush half of glaze over cake, letting it soak in for about 10 minutes. Brush remaining glaze over cake. Cool completely before cutting cake.

Pistachio Fudge Marble Cake

Preheat oven to 350°F (180°C)
10-inch (4 L) tube pan, greased and floured

SERVES 12 TO 16

The unusual combination of a pale green cake with chocolate swirls is both attractive and delicious.

Tips

For a potluck party, bake the cake in a 13- by 9-inch (3 L) pan for 35 minutes and serve individual pieces with a spoonful of the frosting on top.

Use the green food coloring to suit your taste. The pudding by itself will give a hint of green. Added coloring will create more vibrancy.

CAKE

1	pkg (18.25 oz/515 g) fudge marble cake mix	1
1	pkg (4-serving size) pistachio instant pudding mix	1
4	eggs	4
1 cup	water	250 mL
1/3 cup	vegetable oil	75 mL
5 drops	green food coloring, optional	5 drops

FROSTING

1	pkg (4-serving size) pistachio instant pudding mix	1
2	envelopes (each 1 1/2 oz/42.5 g) dessert topping mix	2
1 1/4 cups	cold milk	300 mL
	Green food coloring, optional	
	Chocolate curls or shaved chocolate, optional	

1. **Cake:** In a large mixer bowl, combine large cake mix packet, pudding mix, eggs, water and oil. Beat on medium speed for 2 minutes. Stir in food colouring, if desired. Transfer 1 cup (250 mL) batter to another bowl and stir in small cocoa packet from cake mix. Spread half of green batter in prepared pan. Drizzle half of chocolate batter on top. Repeat layers with remaining batters. Run tip of knife through batters to create a marble effect. Bake for 45 to 50 minutes or until a tester inserted in the center comes out clean. Cool 30 minutes in pan on wire rack then remove and cool completely.

2. **Frosting:** In a large mixer bowl, combine pudding mix, whipped topping mixes and milk. Beat on high speed until stiff peaks form, about 3 minutes. Beat in coloring, if desired. Spread frosting on top and sides of cake. Decorate with chocolate, if desired. Chill until serving. Store leftover cake in the refrigerator.

Creamy Orange Cake

Preheat oven to 350°F (180°C)
10-inch (3 L) Bundt or (4 L) tube pan, greased and floured

SERVES 12 TO 16

This delicious cake is memorable for both its bright orange color and its creamy orange taste.

Tip
Two to three oranges (1 lb/500 g) will yield 3 tbsp (45 mL) grated zest and 1 cup (250 mL) juice.

Variation
Try pineapple orange gelatin for a more mellow flavor.

CAKE

1	pkg (18.25 oz/515 g) white cake mix	1
1	pkg (3 oz/85 g) orange gelatin dessert mix	1
1	envelope (1 1/2 oz/42.5 g) dessert topping mix	1
4	eggs	4
3/4 cup	mayonnaise	175 mL
1 tbsp	grated orange zest	15 mL
3/4 cup	orange juice	175 mL

GLAZE

1 cup	confectioner's (icing) sugar, sifted	250 mL
1 tsp	grated orange zest	5 mL
1 tbsp	orange juice	15 mL

1. ***Cake:*** In a large mixer bowl, combine cake mix, gelatin mix, topping mix, eggs, mayonnaise, orange zest and juice. Beat on low speed for 1 minute to blend, then on medium speed for 2 minutes. Spread batter evenly in prepared pan. Bake for 40 to 50 minutes or until a tester inserted in the center comes out clean. Cool in pan on a wire rack for 25 minutes, then remove from pan and place on rack set over waxed paper to cool.

2. ***Glaze:*** In a bowl, combine confectioner's sugar, orange zest and juice, mixing until smooth. Drizzle over cooled cake. Let glaze set before cutting cake.

Coffee Cakes

Raspberry Streusel Coffee Cake

Preheat oven to 375°F (190°C)
13- by 9-inch (3 L) cake pan, greased

SERVES 12 TO 16

Here's a great way to enjoy this delicious fruit when it is in season and at its peak of perfection.

Tip
If the raspberries seem overly juicy, toss then with a little flour before adding to the batter.

Variation
A mixture of blueberries and raspberries or blueberries alone also taste great.

STREUSEL

½ cup	packed brown sugar	125 mL
2 tbsp	all-purpose flour	25 mL
2 tbsp	butter, melted	25 mL
½ tsp	cinnamon	2 mL
¾ cup	sliced hazelnuts	175 mL

CAKE

1	pkg (18.25 oz/515 g) white cake mix	1
⅓ cup	granulated sugar	75 mL
8 oz	cream cheese, softened	250 g
3	eggs	3
½ cup	vegetable oil	125 mL
¼ cup	water	50 mL
2 to 3 cups	fresh raspberries	500 to 750 mL

1. **Streusel:** In a bowl, combine sugar, flour, melted butter, cinnamon and hazelnuts, mixing until crumbly. Set aside.

2. **Cake:** In a large mixer bowl, combine cake mix, sugar, cream cheese, eggs, oil and water. Beat on low speed for 1 minute to blend, then on medium speed for 2 minutes or until smooth. Spread half of batter in prepared pan. Scatter raspberries over batter. Spread remaining batter over berries. Sprinkle streusel evenly over batter. Bake for 40 to 45 minutes or until top springs back when lightly touched. Cool 30 minutes in pan on a wire rack. Serve warm or cool.

Sour Cream Poppy Seed Coffee Cake

Preheat oven to 350°F (180°C)
10-inch (4 L) tube pan, greased and floured

SERVES 12 TO 16

Poppy seeds add a nice crunch to this tender moist cake.

Tips
If you prefer a stronger coffee flavor, use instant espresso coffee powder.

For an attractive finish, dust the top of this cake with confectioner's sugar. A small sieve, salt shaker or spice bottle with holes in the top work well for dusting.

Variation
Add ⅓ cup (75 mL) chopped nuts to the filling.

FILLING

⅓ cup	packed brown sugar	75 mL
2 tsp	ground cinnamon	10 mL
½ tsp	instant coffee powder	2 mL

CAKE

1	pkg (18.25 oz/515 g) white cake mix	1
1	pkg (4-serving size) vanilla instant pudding mix	1
4	eggs	4
1 cup	sour cream	250 mL
½ cup	vegetable oil	125 mL
¼ cup	poppy seeds	50 mL

1. **Filling:** In a small bowl, combine sugar, cinnamon and coffee powder. Set aside.

2. **Cake:** In a large mixer bowl, combine cake mix, pudding mix, eggs, sour cream, oil and poppy seeds. Beat on medium speed for 4 minutes. Spread half of batter in prepared pan. Sprinkle filling mixture evenly over batter. Cover with remaining batter. Bake for 50 to 55 minutes or until a tester inserted in the center comes out clean. Cool 25 minutes in pan on a wire rack, then remove from pan and place on rack. Serve warm or cool.

Apple Pinwheel Cake

Preheat oven to 350°F (180°C)
10$\frac{1}{2}$-inch (26 cm) springform pan, greased

SERVES 12 TO 16

This versatile cake is sure to impress your guests.

Tips
Although this cake is very attractive plain, you can dress it up with a white drizzle and some toasted pecan halves on top. It's also delicious served with a drizzle of caramel sauce and whipped cream.

Golden delicious apples work well in this recipe, as they hold their shape during baking.

Variation
Try other fruits such as pears, plums or nectarines, instead of apples.

TOPPING

4 to 5	apples	4 to 5
1 tbsp	lemon juice	15 mL
1$\frac{1}{2}$ tbsp	granulated sugar	22 mL
1$\frac{1}{2}$ tsp	ground cinnamon	7 mL

CAKE

1	pkg (18.25 oz/515 g) white cake mix	1
$\frac{1}{4}$ cup	granulated sugar	50 mL
8 oz	cream cheese, softened	250 g
3	eggs	3
$\frac{1}{3}$ cup	vegetable oil	75 mL
$\frac{1}{4}$ cup	water	50 mL
1 tsp	ground cinnamon	5 mL

1. ***Topping:*** Peel, core and thinly slice apples to make 4 cups (1 L). Toss with lemon juice. Set aside. In a separate bowl, combine sugar and cinnamon. Set aside.

2. ***Cake:*** In a large mixer bowl, combine cake mix, sugar, cream cheese, eggs, oil, water and cinnamon. Beat on low speed for 1 minute to blend, then on medium speed for 2 minutes. Spread batter evenly in prepared pan. Arrange apple slices attractively on top of batter, overlapping slightly as necessary. Sprinkle with cinnamon-sugar mixture. Bake for 60 to 70 minutes or until a tester inserted in the center of cake portion comes out clean. Cool 30 minutes in pan on a wire rack. Serve warm or cool.

Apple Nut Coffee Cake

Preheat oven to 350°F (180°C)
13- by 9-inch (3 L) cake pan, greased

SERVES 12 TO 16

This easy one-step cake has a delicious baked-on topping.

Tip
Use the medium coarse grater size for the apples. The cake will be too moist if the apples are too finely grated.

Variations
Substitute firm pears for the apples.

Try adding 1 tbsp (15 mL) grated orange zest to the batter.

CAKE

1	pkg (18.25 oz/515 g) white cake mix	1
3	eggs	3
1/2 cup	water	125 mL
1/3 cup	vegetable oil	75 mL
2 cups	grated peeled apples (3 large apples)	500 mL

TOPPING

1/2 cup	packed brown sugar	125 mL
1/2 cup	chopped nuts	125 mL
1 tsp	ground cinnamon	5 mL
1 tbsp	butter, melted	15 mL

1. *Cake:* In a large mixer bowl, combine cake mix, eggs, water and oil. Beat on medium speed for 2 minutes. Stir in apples, mixing until thoroughly blended. Spread batter evenly in prepared pan.

2. *Topping:* In a bowl, combine brown sugar, nuts, cinnamon and melted butter. Mix well. Sprinkle evenly over batter. Bake for 35 to 45 minutes or until a tester inserted in the center comes out clean. Cool 30 minutes in pan on a wire rack. Serve warm or cool.

Crunchy White Chocolate Banana Coffee Cake

Preheat oven to 350°F (180°C)
13- by 9-inch (3 L) cake pan, greased

SERVES 12 TO 16

This cake is very simple, yet very good.

Tip
Cakes baked in this size pan are usually frosted and served from the pan, which makes them easy to transport. If you want to remove the entire cake from the pan, line it with foil, leaving an overhang on the sides. You'll be able to lift the cooled cake out easily.

Variations
Try substituting a butterscotch or chocolate pudding for the vanilla. They make an interesting combination with banana.

Omit topping. Spread Banana Butter Frosting (see recipe, page 179) over cooled cake.

CAKE

1	pkg (18.25 oz/515 g) white cake mix	1
1	pkg (4-serving size) vanilla instant pudding mix	1
4	eggs	4
1 1/4 cups	mashed ripe bananas (3 large bananas)	300 mL
1/3 cup	vegetable oil	75 mL
1 cup	white chocolate chips	250 mL

TOPPING

3/4 cup	chopped almonds	175 mL
1/2 cup	packed brown sugar	125 mL
2 tbsp	butter, melted	25 mL

1. **Cake:** In a large mixer bowl, combine cake mix, pudding mix, eggs, mashed bananas and oil. Beat on medium speed for 2 minutes. Stir in white chocolate chips. Spread batter evenly in prepared pan.

2. **Topping:** In a bowl, combine almonds, brown sugar and melted butter. Mix well. Sprinkle evenly over batter. Bake for 35 to 40 minutes or until a tester inserted in the center comes out clean. Cool 30 minutes in pan on a wire rack. Serve warm or cool.

Chocolate Banana Coffee Cake

Preheat oven to 350°F (180°C)
13- by 9-inch (3 L) cake pan, greased

SERVES 12 TO 16

This moist cake is easy to make and keeps well. It is perfect for a lunchbox treat or after-school snack.

Tip
Store overly ripe bananas in the freezer, skin and all, until you have enough to use in a recipe.

Variations
Try using regular chocolate chips in place of the miniature version for a chunkier top.

For a stronger banana flavor, use a banana cream instant pudding mix instead of the vanilla.

TOPPING

½ cup	packed brown sugar	125 mL
1 tsp	ground cinnamon	5 mL
1½ cups	miniature semi-sweet chocolate chips	375 mL

CAKE

1	pkg (18.25 oz/515 g) devil's food cake mix	1
1	pkg (4-serving size) vanilla instant pudding mix	1
4	eggs	4
1½ cups	mashed ripe bananas (3 to 4 large bananas)	375 mL
⅓ cup	vegetable oil	75 mL

1. **Topping:** In a small bowl, combine brown sugar and cinnamon. Set aside.

2. **Cake:** In a large mixer bowl, combine cake mix, pudding mix, eggs, mashed bananas and oil. Beat on medium speed for 2 minutes. Spread half of batter in prepared pan. Sprinkle half of topping over batter in pan. Sprinkle with half of the chocolate chips. Repeat layers with remaining cake batter, topping and chips. Bake for 45 to 50 minutes or until a tester inserted in the center comes out clean. Cool 30 minutes in pan on a wire rack. Serve warm or cool.

Cranberry Almond Coffee Cake

Preheat oven to 350°F (180°C)
13- by 9-inch (3 L) cake pan, greased

SERVES 12 TO 16

Don't limit this cake to the holiday season. The tart cranberry taste and crunchy almond top are a hit year round.

Tip
When cranberries are in season, buy a few bags for your freezer. Thaw slightly before using and, if they seem quite moist, pat dry and toss with a bit of flour before adding to the batter.

Variation
Replace cranberries with fresh blueberries or raspberries.

CAKE

2 cups	fresh cranberries	500 mL
¼ cup	all-purpose flour	50 mL
1	pkg (18.25 oz/515 g) white cake mix	1
3	eggs	3
1¼ cups	water	300 mL
⅓ cup	vegetable oil	75 mL
½ tsp	almond extract	2 mL

TOPPING

¾ cup	sliced almonds	175 mL
⅓ cup	packed brown sugar	75 mL
½ tsp	ground cinnamon	2 mL

1. **Cake:** In a small bowl, toss cranberries in flour to coat well. In a large mixer bowl, combine cake mix, eggs, water, oil and almond extract. Beat for 2 minutes on medium speed. Stir in floured cranberries. Spread batter evenly in prepared pan.

2. **Topping:** In a small bowl, combine almonds, brown sugar and cinnamon. Mix well. Sprinkle evenly over batter. Bake for 30 to 40 minutes or until a tester inserted in the center comes out clean. Cool 30 minutes in pan on a wire rack. Serve warm or cool.

Quick Breads & Muffins

White Chocolate Cranberry Loaf

Preheat oven to 350°F (180°C)
Two 8¹/₂- by 4¹/₂-inch (1.5 L) loaf pans, greased and floured

MAKES ABOUT
30 SLICES

This recipe makes 2 loaves. Enjoy 1 fresh and freeze the other to serve if company drops in unexpectedly.

Tips
Keep a few bags of cranberries in the freezer for year round use.

Use 1 cup (250 mL) of white chocolate chips instead of a chopped bar of chocolate.

Variation
Replace cranberries with blueberries or raspberries.

1	pkg (18.25 oz/515 g) white cake mix	1
¾ cup	all-purpose flour, divided	175 mL
3	eggs	3
¾ cup	water	175 mL
1 tbsp	grated orange zest	15 mL
½ cup	orange juice	125 mL
⅓ cup	vegetable oil	75 mL
1 cup	fresh cranberries	250 mL
1 cup	chopped white chocolate	250 mL

1. In a large mixer bowl, combine cake mix, ½ cup (125 mL) of the flour, eggs, water, orange zest and juice and oil. Beat on low speed for 1 minute to blend, then on medium speed for 2 minutes. Toss cranberries in remaining flour to coat thoroughly. Stir into batter with chocolate. Spread batter in prepared pans, dividing evenly. Bake for 50 to 60 minutes or until a tester inserted in the center comes out clean. Cool 20 minutes in pans on a wire rack, then remove from pans and cool completely on rack.

Apple Carrot Oatmeal Muffins

Preheat oven to 375°F (190°C)
One 12-cup and one 6-cup muffin tin, greased or paper-lined

MAKES 18 MUFFINS

Here's a delicious way to enjoy your vegetables.

Tip
Be sure to peel the carrots before grating them for use in this recipe. The reaction of the peel with the leavening in the batter can form green specks.

Variation
For a different flavor, replace raisins with dried cranberries or dried cherries.

1	pkg (18.25 oz/515 g) white cake mix	1
1 1/2 cups	quick-cooking oats	375 mL
2 tsp	ground cinnamon	10 mL
1/2 tsp	baking powder	2 mL
3	eggs	3
1 1/4 cups	peeled, grated apples (2 large apples)	300 mL
1 1/4 cups	peeled, grated carrots	300 mL
1 1/4 cups	milk	300 mL
1/2 cup	butter, melted	125 mL
3/4 cup	raisins	175 mL
3/4 cup	chopped nuts	175 mL

1. In a large bowl, combine cake mix, oats, cinnamon and baking powder. Stir to blend. In another large bowl, whisk together eggs, apples, carrots, milk and melted butter. Add dry ingredients, stirring with a wooden spoon just until blended. Stir in raisins and nuts. Spoon batter into prepared muffin tins. Bake for 20 to 25 minutes or until tops spring back when lightly touched. Cool 15 minutes in pans on a wire rack then remove from pan and cool completely on rack.

Chocolate Banana Muffins

Preheat oven to 375°F (190°C)
Two 12-cup muffin tins, greased or paper-lined

MAKES 24 MUFFINS

This combination of banana and chocolate is one of my favorites.

Tip
These muffins are so tender and moist that you don't need paper liners. Cool them completely in the pans, then loosen with the tip of a knife, and they'll come out in one piece.

Variation
Replace mini chips with regular size or try peanut butter chips for a different flavor.

1	pkg (18.25 oz/515 g) devil's food cake mix	1
1	pkg (4-serving size) banana cream instant pudding mix	1
3	eggs	3
1 1/2 cups	mashed ripe bananas (3 to 4 large bananas)	375 mL
1/4 cup	vegetable oil	50 mL
1 1/3 cups	miniature semi-sweet chocolate chips	325 mL

1. In a large mixer bowl, combine cake mix, pudding mix, eggs, mashed bananas and oil. Stir with wooden spoon just until blended. Fold in chocolate chips. Spoon batter into prepared muffin tins. Bake for 15 to 20 minutes or until set and golden. Cool for 15 minutes in pans on a wire rack then remove from pans and cool completely on rack.

Apple Carrot Oatmeal Muffins (*page 95*) and ▶
Chocolate Banana Muffins (*page 96*)
Overleaf: Chocolate Coffee Marble Cheesecake (*page 118*)

Chocolate Cheesecake Muffins

Preheat oven to 350°F (180°C)
Two 12-cup muffin tins, greased or paper-lined

MAKES 24 MUFFINS

These are definitely not "healthy" breakfast muffins. In fact, they can double as dessert.

Tip
Paper muffin-cup liners make for easy cleanup of the pan. They are also excellent to use if you are transporting or freezing muffins.

Variation
For the flavor of Black Forest cake, replace half the water with cherry liqueur.

FILLING

8 oz	cream cheese, softened	250 g
1	egg	1
1/3 cup	granulated sugar	75 mL
2/3 cup	miniature semi-sweet chocolate chips	150 mL

MUFFIN BATTER

1	pkg (18.25 oz/515 g) devil's food cake mix	1
1	pkg (4-serving size) chocolate instant pudding mix	1
4	eggs	4
1 cup	sour cream	250 mL
1/2 cup	water	125 mL
1/3 cup	vegetable oil	75 mL

1. **Filling:** In a small bowl, beat cream cheese, egg and sugar until smooth. Stir in chocolate chips. Set aside.

2. **Muffin Batter:** In a large mixer bowl, combine cake mix, pudding mix, eggs, sour cream, water and oil. Beat on low speed for 1 minute to blend, then on medium speed for 1 minute. Spoon half of batter into prepared muffin tins. Put about 1 tbsp (15 mL) cheese filling mixture on top. Spoon remaining batter over filling. Bake for 20 to 25 minutes or until top springs back when lightly touched. Cool 15 minutes in pans on a wire rack then remove from pans and cool completely on rack.

◄ Peachy Angel Dessert (*page 103*)

Banana Berry Loaf

Preheat oven to 350°F (180°C)
Two 8½- by 4½-inch (1.5 L) loaf pans, greased and floured

MAKES ABOUT
30 SLICES

Banana adds an enticing flavor to traditional plain cranberry bread.

Tips
Quick breads freeze beautifully. Wrap completely in plastic wrap or air-tight freezer bags or wrap individual slices in plastic and freeze for up to 3 months.

Try a thick slice of this bread, warm with vanilla sauce for dessert.

Variations
Add 1 tbsp (15 mL) grated orange zest to batter.

For a milder vanilla flavor, use a vanilla pudding mix.

1	pkg (18.25 oz/515 g) white cake mix	1
1	pkg (4-serving size) banana cream instant pudding mix	1
4	eggs	4
1½ cups	mashed ripe bananas (3 to 4 large bananas)	375 mL
¼ cup	vegetable oil	50 mL
1½ cups	fresh cranberries	375 mL
2 tbsp	all-purpose flour	25 mL

1. In a large mixer bowl, combine cake mix, pudding mix, eggs, bananas and oil. Beat on low speed for 1 minute to blend, then on medium speed for 2 minutes. Toss cranberries in flour to coat. Fold into batter. Spread batter in prepared pans, dividing evenly. Bake for 50 to 60 minutes or until a tester inserted in the center comes out clean. Cool 20 minutes in pans on a wire rack then remove from pan and cool completely on rack.

Spicy Apple 'n' Oats Loaf

Preheat oven to 350°F (180°C)
Two 8$\frac{1}{2}$- by 4$\frac{1}{2}$-inch (1.5 L) loaf pans, greased and floured

MAKES ABOUT 30 SLICES

Here's a great way to enjoy fruit and cereal for breakfast.

1	pkg (18.25 oz/515 g) spice cake mix	1
$\frac{1}{2}$ cup	quick-cooking oats	125 mL
3	eggs	3
1$\frac{1}{2}$ cups	applesauce	375 mL
$\frac{1}{3}$ cup	vegetable oil	75 mL
1 cup	raisins, dried cranberries or dried cherries	250 mL

Tips

Lightly toasting oats until they are golden gives them a nutty flavor.

If using homemade applesauce that is chunky, press out most of the lumps with a potato masher. Use sweetened or unsweetened, depending on your preference.

For a delicious snack, toast a slice of this bread and sprinkle it with cinnamon-sugar.

Variation

Sprinkle 2 tbsp (25 mL) of toasted oats over top before baking.

1. In a large mixer bowl, combine cake mix, oats, eggs, applesauce and oil. Beat on low speed for 1 minute to blend, then on medium speed for 2 minutes. Stir in raisins. Spread batter in prepared pans, dividing evenly. Bake for 50 to 60 minutes or until a tester inserted in the center comes out clean. Cool 20 minutes in pans on a wire rack, then remove from pan and cool completely on rack.

Lemon Blueberry Loaf

Preheat oven to 350°F (180°C)
Two 8½- by 4½-inch (1.5 L) loaf pans, greased and floured

**MAKES ABOUT
30 SLICES**

*When fresh
blueberries are
in season, prepare
a few extra loaves
of this tasty treat
for the freezer.*

Tips
When using cream
cheese in baking
recipes, make
sure it is at room
temperature for
easy blending.

To serve this as a
dessert cake, frost
with Lemon Butter
Cream (see recipe,
page 171) or Very
Creamy Butter
Frosting, flavoured
with lemon (see
recipe, page 172).

Variation
Replace blueberries
with cranberries
and hazelnuts with
almonds or pecans.

1¼ cups	fresh blueberries	300 mL
¾ cup	sliced hazelnuts	175 mL
1 tbsp	all-purpose flour	15 mL
1	pkg (18.25 oz/515 g) lemon cake mix	1
4	eggs	4
4 oz	cream cheese, softened	125 g
⅔ cup	milk	150 mL

1. Toss blueberries and nuts with flour to coat. Set aside.

2. In a large mixer bowl, combine cake mix, eggs, cream cheese and milk. Beat on low speed for 1 minute to blend, then on medium speed for 2 minutes. Fold in blueberry mixture. Spread batter in prepared pans, dividing evenly. Bake for 45 to 50 minutes or until a tester inserted in the center comes out clean. Cool 20 minutes in pans on a wire rack then remove from pan and cool completely on rack.

Angel Food Cakes

Tiramisu Angel Torte

Preheat oven to 325°F (160°C)
10-inch (4 L) tube pan, ungreased

SERVES 12 TO 16

Traditionally made with ladyfingers, this angel food version is lighter than the classic Italian dessert.

Tips
For an even richer flavor, substitute traditional marscapone cheese for the cream cheese.

If desired, substitute 1 tbsp (15 mL) coffee powder for the espresso powder.

Variations
Use ¼ cup (50 mL) coffee liqueur or crème de cacao with an equal quantity of amaretto.

Use semi-sweet chocolate in place of bittersweet.

CAKE

1	pkg (16 oz/450 g) white angel food cake mix	1

FILLING & FROSTING

8 oz	cream cheese, softened	250 g
2 cups	whipping (35%) cream, divided	500 mL
⅔ cup	confectioner's (icing) sugar, sifted	150 mL
½ cup	almond liqueur (Amaretto), divided	125 mL
3 tbsp	unsweetened cocoa powder, sifted	45 mL
1 tbsp	instant espresso powder	15 mL
3 oz	bittersweet chocolate, coarsely grated	90 g
1 cup	sliced almonds, toasted	250 mL
	Chocolate curls or shavings, optional	

1. ***Cake:*** Prepare cake according to package directions. With a long sharp serrated knife, cut cake horizontally into 3 layers.

2. ***Filling:*** In a large mixer bowl, beat cream cheese until smooth. Add 1 cup (250 mL) of cream, confectioner's sugar, 2 tbsp (25 mL) of liqueur, cocoa and coffee powder. Beat until smooth. In a separate bowl, beat remaining cream to stiff peaks. Fold into cheese mixture.

3. ***Assembly:*** Place bottom cake layer, cut-side up on a serving plate. Sprinkle with 2 tbsp (30 mL) of liqueur. Spread with 1 cup (250 mL) of filling. Sprinkle with half of chocolate. Repeat layer. Top with third cake layer, cut-side down. Sprinkle with liqueur. Cover top and sides with remaining filling. Press almonds onto sides. Decorate top with chocolate curls. Chill until serving. Store in refrigerator.

Peachy Angel Dessert

Preheat oven to 325°F (160°C)
10-inch (4 L) tube pan, ungreased
13- by 9-inch (3 L) cake pan, ungreased

SERVES 12 TO 16

This versatile make-ahead dessert is ideal for potluck parties.

Tip
If it's more convenient, you can prepare the cake a few days ahead.

Variation
Use your favorite pie filling and choose a complimentary liqueur.

CAKE

1	pkg (16 oz/450 g) white angel food cake mix	1

FILLING

8 oz	cream cheese, softened	250 g
1 cup	confectioner's (icing) sugar, sifted	250 mL
2 cups	whipping (35%) cream	500 mL
¼ cup	peach schnapps liqueur	50 mL
1	can (19 oz/540 mL) peach pie filling	1

1. **Cake:** Prepare, bake and cool cake according to package directions. Tear into bite-size pieces. Set aside.

2. **Filling:** In a large mixer bowl, beat cream cheese and confectioner's sugar until light and fluffy. In a separate bowl, beat whipping cream and liqueur to stiff peaks. Fold cream mixture into cheese mixture, gently but thoroughly. Add cake pieces. Stir well to evenly coat cake with filling. Spoon into rectangle cake pan. Press down lightly. Spread pie filling over top. Chill until serving. Store leftover dessert in the refrigerator.

Coffee Almond Angel Dessert

Preheat oven to 325°F (160°C)
10-inch (4 L) tube pan, ungreased
Large rimmed baking sheet, greased

SERVES 12 TO 16

This is definitely the dessert to choose, if you're trying to impress.

Tips
When making the sugared almonds, use a baking sheet with sides or a jellyroll pan so you can stir them easily. Non-stick sheets work well.

Prepare sugared almonds 1 or 2 days ahead. Store in a cookie tin at room temperature.

Chocolate drizzle makes this cake even more sophisticated.

Variation
Omit almond extract or replace with vanilla, if desired.

CAKE

1	pkg (16 oz/450 g) white angel food cake mix	1
2 tbsp	instant coffee powder	25 mL
1/2 tsp	almond extract	2 mL

FROSTING

2 cups	whipping (35%) cream	500 mL
1/4 cup	confectioner's (icing) sugar, sifted	50 mL
1 tbsp	instant coffee powder	15 mL
1/2 tsp	almond extract	2 mL

SUGARED ALMOND GARNISH

1 1/2 cups	sliced almonds	375 mL
1/3 cup	granulated sugar	75 mL
2 tbsp	water	25 mL

1. **Cake:** Add coffee powder and almond extract to cake mix and prepare, bake and cool according to package directions.

2. **Frosting:** In a large mixer bowl, combine whipping cream, confectioner's sugar, coffee powder and almond extract. Beat to stiff peaks. Spread on top and sides of cake.

3. **Sugared Almonds:** Preheat oven to 350°F (180°C). In a bowl, combine almonds, sugar and water. Stir well to thoroughly coat nuts. Spread on prepared baking sheet. Bake for 12 to 15 minutes, stirring often, until golden. Remove from oven. Immediately loosen from baking sheet, then cool completely in pan on a wire rack. Break into clusters. Press nuts over top and sides of cake. Refrigerate until serving. Store leftover cake in the refrigerator.

Crunchy Chocolate Toffee Angel Cake

Preheat oven to 325°F (160°C)
10-inch (4 L) tue pan, ungreased

Tips
Freeze chocolate
bars before crushing.
Leave in package
and hit with mallet
to crush.

Chill bowl and beater
before whipping
cream to get
maximum volume.

Variation
Add 3 tbsp (45 mL)
sifted unsweetened
cocoa powder to dry
cake mix for a
chocolate cake.

CAKE

1	pkg (16 oz/450 g) white angel food cake mix	1

FILLING & TOPPING

3 cups	whipping (35%) cream	750 mL
6	toffee-crunch chocolate bars (each 1.4 oz/39 g)	6

1. **Cake:** Prepare, bake and cool cake according to package directions. With an electric knife or long, sharp serrated knife, cut cake horizontally into 2 or 3 layers.

2. **Filling & Topping:** In a large mixer bowl, beat cream to stiff peaks. Finely crush 5 of the chocolate bars. Chop the last bar into larger pieces. Fold the finely-crushed bars into the whipped cream. Place 1 cake layer cut-side up on serving plate. Spread with 1 cup (250 mL) of the cream. Repeat with remaining cake layers and cream, ending with a cake layer, cut-side down. Spread remaining cream over sides and top of cake. Sprinkle coarsely-chopped bar on top. Chill until serving. Store leftover cake in the refrigerator.

Lemon Angel Torte

Preheat oven to 325°F (160°C)
10-inch (4 L) tube pan, ungreased

SERVES 12 TO 16

A tart lemon cream filling between layers of angel food cake makes for a mouthwatering dessert.

Tips
If you prefer or can't find canned lemon pie filling, prepare a cooked lemon pie filling. Cool before using.

An electric knife is ideal to slice angel food and chiffon cakes.

Chill the cake at least 4 hours before serving to allow the flavors to blend.

Variation
Crushed hard lemon candies sprinkled on top of the cake add a nice crunch to the lemon cream.

CAKE

1	pkg (16 oz/450 g) white angel food cake mix	1
1 tbsp	grated lemon zest	15 mL

LEMON CREAM FILLING & TOPPING

1 cup	whipping (35%) cream	250 mL
1 tbsp	confectioner's (icing) sugar	15 mL
1	can (19 oz/540 mL) prepared lemon pie filling ($2\frac{1}{4}$ cups/550 mL)	1
	Lemon twists, optional	

1. **Cake:** Add lemon zest to cake mix and prepare, bake and cool according to package directions. With electric knife or long sharp serrated knife, cut cake horizontally into 3 layers.

2. **Filling:** In a large mixer bowl, beat cream and confectioner's sugar to stiff peaks. Fold in pie filling, gently but thoroughly. Place one cake layer, cut-side up on serving plate. Spread 1 cup (250 mL) of the filling on cake. Repeat with remaining cake layers and filling, ending with cake layer, cut-side down. Spread remaining filling on sides and top of cake. Chill at least 4 hours before serving. Garnish with lemon twists, if desired. Store leftover cake in the refrigerator.

Pink Coconut Cake

Preheat oven to 325°F (160°C)
10-inch (4 L) tube pan, ungreased

SERVES 10

A simple decoration makes this cake special.

Tip
You can change the color of coconut and make it pastel or bright, depending on the amount of color used.

Variation
Omit coloring. Use toasted coconut instead of plain in both the cake and topping.

CAKE

| 1 | pkg (16 oz /450 g) white angel food cake mix | 1 |
| 2/3 cup | flaked coconut | 150 mL |

TOPPING

2 cups	whipping (35%) cream	500 mL
1/4 cup	confectioner's (icing) sugar, sifted	50 mL
2/3 cup	flaked coconut	150 mL
5	drops red food coloring	5

1. **Cake:** Prepare cake mix according to package directions. Fold in coconut. Bake and cool as directed.

2. **Topping:** In a large mixer bowl, beat whipping cream and confectioner's sugar to stiff peaks. Place cake upside-down on a serving plate. Frost completely with cream. Shake coconut and food coloring in tightly covered jar until coconut is evenly tinted a delicate pink. Mark top and sides of cake into 10 equal wedges and side panels. Sprinkle pink coconut over alternate wedges on top and side panels. Each serving will have coconut on either the top or the side. Chill until serving. Store leftover cake in refrigerator.

Raspberry Angel Trifle

Preheat oven to 325°F (160°C)
10-inch (4 L) tube pan, ungreased
Trifle bowl or large glass serving bowl.

SERVES 12 TO 16

This delicious cake is sure to become a tradition for special occasions such as Christmas and Mother's Day.

Tips
You can use frozen berries in place of fresh. Keep in mind they will be juicy so the pudding will be pinkish and the texture much moister.

Prepare custard and cake the day before the trifle is to be served.

Refer to Ingredients chapter to melt chocolate.

Variation
A mixture of berries also works well in this recipe. Strawberries, blackberries and blueberries are always popular.

CAKE

1	pkg (16 oz/450 g) white angel food cake mix	1

CUSTARD

4	egg yolks	4
¼ cup	granulated sugar	50 mL
¾ cup	all-purpose flour	175 mL
3 cups	milk	750 mL

FILLING

2 cups	whipping (35%) cream	500 mL
¼ cup	orange liqueur	50 mL
3 cups	fresh raspberries	750 mL

GARNISH

3 tbsp	toasted, sliced almonds	45 mL
1 oz	semi-sweet chocolate, melted, optional	30 g

1. **Cake:** Prepare, bake and cool cake according to package directions. Cut cake in half. Reserve half in freezer for your next dessert request. Tear remaining half into bite-size pieces. Set aside.

2. **Custard:** In a large saucepan, combine egg yolks, sugar, flour and milk. Cook, over medium heat, stirring constantly until thickened, about 5 minutes. Cover tightly with plastic wrap pressing against the surface to prevent a skin from forming. Chill thoroughly.

3. **Filling:** In a large mixer bowl, beat whipping cream and liqueur to stiff peaks. Fold half of cream mixture into custard.

4. Assembly: Spread half of custard filling in trifle bowl. Put half of cake pieces on top. Sprinkle half of berries over cake. Repeat layers with remaining custard filling, cake and berries. Spread remaining whipped cream on top. Sprinkle almonds on top and drizzle with melted chocolate, if desired. Store leftover dessert in the refrigerator.

Pineapple Angel Delight

Preheat oven to 325°F (160°C)
13- by 9-inch (3 L) cake pan, ungreased

SERVES ABOUT 12

It's embarrassing to admit how easy it is to make this fantastic cake.

Tip
Garnish plate with fresh pineapple chunks or slices.

Variation
Add grated orange zest or coconut extract to the batter.

1	pkg (16 oz/450 g) white angel food cake mix	1
1	can (19 oz/540 mL) crushed pineapple, including juice	1
	Whipped cream, optional	

1. In a large mixer bowl, combine cake mix and crushed pineapple, including juice. Beat on low speed for 30 seconds to blend, then on medium speed for 1 minute. Pour into pan. Bake for 30 to 35 minutes or until top is brown and firm. Cool completely in pan on a wire rack. Cover top with whipped cream or serve individual pieces with a generous scoop of ice cream.

Cheesecakes

Caramel Cashew Cheesecake

Preheat oven to 325°F (160°C)
10-inch (25 cm) springform pan, greased

SERVES 12 TO 16

This dessert is a knock-out — it will dazzle your guests.

Tips
The topping looks amazing but the taste of this cake is so good that it works as a plain cheesecake, too.

The filling puffs during baking and settles on cooling.

Don't overbeat cheesecake fillings. This can cause them to crack during baking.

Variation
Omit topping. Serve with a drizzle of caramel or chocolate sauce.

CRUST

1	pkg (18.25 oz/515 g) white cake mix	1
¾ cup	finely chopped roasted, unsalted cashews	175 mL
⅓ cup	butter, melted	75 mL
1	egg	1

FILLING

1½ lbs	cream cheese, softened	750 g
1 cup	granulated sugar	250 mL
4	eggs	4
¼ cup	whipping (35%) cream	50 mL
2 tsp	vanilla	10 mL

TOPPING

1 cup	granulated sugar	250 mL
3 tbsp	water	45 mL
⅔ cup	whipping (35%) cream	150 mL
1 cup	roasted, unsalted cashews, coarsely chopped	250 mL

1. **Crust:** In a large mixer bowl, combine cake mix, cashews, melted butter and egg. Beat on low speed for 1 minute or until soft, moist dough forms. Press evenly over bottom and 1½ inches (3.5 cm) up sides of prepared pan. Chill while preparing filling.

2. **Filling:** In a large mixer bowl, beat cream cheese and sugar on medium speed until smooth. Add eggs, 1 at a time, beating well after each addition. Add cream and vanilla, beating just until blended. Pour filling into prepared crust. Bake for 70 to 80 minutes or just until edges are set and the center has a slight jiggle to it. Run knife around edge of pan to loosen cake. Cool completely on a wire rack.

3. **_Topping:_** In a saucepan, over low heat, heat sugar and water, stirring constantly, until sugar dissolves. Increase heat to medium-high and boil swirling the pan often until the mixture turns amber, about 10 minutes. Carefully add cream (mixture will bubble up). Bring to a simmer, stirring until smooth. Remove from heat. Stir in cashews. Cool to lukewarm. Carefully spoon topping over cheesecake. Chill overnight or up to 3 days before serving. Let stand at room temperature 1 hour before cutting. Store in the refrigerator.

No-Bake Bumbleberry Cheesecake

Preheat oven to 350°F (180°C)
10-inch (25 cm) springform pan, greased

SERVES 12 TO 16

This light but creamy cheesecake is bursting with fresh berry flavor.

Tip
I prefer regular cream cheese for baked cheesecake but the light is well suited to unbaked versions and works well with other light ingredients such as fresh berries.

Variation
Use your favorite berries as long as the total amount is 3½ cups (825 mL). Blackberries are nice in season.

CRUST

1	pkg (18.25 oz/515 g) white cake mix	1
⅓ cup	butter, melted	75 mL
1	egg	1

FILLING

1	envelope (¼ oz/7 g or 1 tbsp/15 mL) unflavored gelatin	1
¼ cup	cold water	50 mL
1 lb	cream cheese, softened	500 g
1 cup	granulated sugar	250 mL
2 tbsp	lemon juice	25 mL
1½ cups	whipping (35%) cream	375 mL
1½ cups	fresh strawberries, crushed	375 mL
1 cup	fresh blueberries, crushed	250 mL
1 cup	fresh raspberries, crushed	250 mL

GARNISH

1 cup	whipping (35%) cream	250 mL
¼ cup	confectioner's (icing) sugar, sifted	50 mL
1 cup	mixed whole berries	250 mL

1. **Crust:** In a large mixer bowl, combine cake mix, melted butter and egg. Beat on low speed for 1 minute or until a soft, moist dough forms. Press firmly in bottom of pan. Bake for 10 to 15 minutes or until golden. Cool in pan on a wire rack.

2. ***Filling:*** Sprinkle gelatin over water in small saucepan. Let stand for 2 minutes. Heat over low heat, stirring until dissolved. Remove from heat. Set aside to cool slightly. Combine cream cheese and sugar in large mixer bowl. Beat on medium speed for 3 minutes or until light and creamy. Gradually add gelatin mixture and lemon juice, beating until smooth. In a separate mixer bowl, beat cream to soft peaks. Fold into cheese mixture. Fold in crushed berries, gently but thoroughly. Pour over crust. Chill until firm, about 2 hours or overnight.

3. ***Garnish:*** In a large mixer bowl, beat cream and confectioner's sugar until stiff peaks form. Pipe rosettes around top of cheesecake and garnish with fresh berries. Store in the refrigerator.

Dutch Apple Crumble Cheesecake

Preheat oven to 350°F (180°C)
10-inch (25 cm) springform pan, greased

SERVES 12 TO 16

Replace the pie part of Dutch apple pie with cheesecake and you've really got a winner.

Tips
To soften hard, lumpy brown sugar, put a slice of apple in the bag and leave it for a few days. For immediate results, put apple and brown sugar in a microwave-safe bowl. Cover and heat on high for 30 seconds. Remove apple and stir.

Variation
Replace apple with a nectarine or pear or a mixture.

CRUST

1	pkg (18.25 oz/515 g) white cake mix, divided	1
½ cup	butter, melted	125 mL

TOPPING

¼ cup	packed brown sugar	50 mL
¾ tsp	ground cinnamon	3 mL
2 tbsp	butter, softened	25 mL

FILLING

1½ lbs	cream cheese, softened	750 g
1 cup	packed brown sugar	250 mL
1 cup	sour cream	250 mL
4	eggs	4
2 tsp	vanilla	10 mL
1 tsp	ground cinnamon	5 mL
½ tsp	ground nutmeg	2 mL
¼ tsp	ground cloves	1 mL
1	large apple, peeled, cored and cut in ¼-inch (1 cm) slices (about 16 slices)	1

1. **Crust:** Reserve ⅓ cup (75 mL) cake mix for topping. Combine remaining cake mix with melted butter. Mix well until a soft dough forms. Press evenly over bottom and 1 inch (2.5 cm) up sides of prepared pan. Bake for 8 to 10 minutes or until starting to set but still soft and not golden. Cool in pan on a wire rack.

2. **Topping:** In a bowl, combine reserved cake mix, brown sugar, cinnamon and butter, mixing until crumbly. Set aside.

116

3. **Filling:** In a large mixer bowl, combine cream cheese, brown sugar and sour cream. Beat on medium speed for 3 minutes. Add eggs, 1 at a time, beating well after each addition. Beat in vanilla, cinnamon, nutmeg and cloves. Pour filling into prepared crust. Arrange apple slices on top in a circular pattern, overlapping slightly as necessary. Sprinkle topping evenly over apples. Bake for 50 to 60 minutes or just until edges are set and the center has a slight jiggle to it. Run knife around edge of pan to loosen cake. Cool completely on a wire rack. Cover and refrigerate overnight before cutting. Store in the refrigerator.

Chocolate Coffee Marble Cheesecake

Preheat oven to 350°F (180°C)
10-inch (25 cm) springform pan, greased

CRUST

1	pkg (18.25 oz/515 g) devil's food cake mix	1
1/3 cup	butter, melted	75 mL
1	egg	1

FILLING

1 1/2 lbs	cream cheese, softened	750 g
1 cup	granulated sugar	250 mL
3	eggs	3
2 tbsp	instant coffee powder, dissolved in 1 tbsp (15 mL) hot water	25 mL
1/4 cup	butter, melted and cooled	50 mL
6 oz	bittersweet chocolate, chopped	175 g
1/4 cup	whipping (35%) cream	50 mL

1. **Crust:** In a large mixer bowl, combine cake mix, melted butter and egg. Beat on low speed until dough forms. Press evenly over bottom and 1 inch (2.5 cm) up sides of prepared pan. Chill while preparing filling.

2. **Filling:** In a large mixer bowl, beat cream cheese and sugar on medium speed until smooth. Add eggs, 1 at a time, beating well after each addition. Add coffee mixture and melted butter. Mix well. In a saucepan on low heat, melt chocolate with cream. Pour half of cheese filling (about 2 1/2 cups/625 mL) into prepared crust. Drop 5 large spoonfuls of chocolate mixture around the edge, spacing evenly. Run tip of knife, through batters to create a marble effect. Pour remaining cheese filling on top and drop spoonfuls of chocolate mixture into the center 6 inches (15 cm) of filling, spacing evenly. Swirl to create a marble effect. Bake for 55 to 65 minutes or just until the center has a slight jiggle to it. Run knife around edge of pan to loosen cake. Cool completely on a wire rack. Store in the refrigerator.

Special Occasion Cakes

Frosty the Snowman Cake

Preheat oven to 350°F (180°C)
One 8-inch (20 cm) and one 9-inch (23 cm) round cake pan, greased and floured
Baking sheets, covered with foil
Cake board or tray (18- by 10-inch/45 by 25 cm), covered in foil

MAKES
1 SNOWMAN CAKE

Let your kids have fun decorating Frosty with their favorite candies.

Tips
Buy a selection of candies. Don't worry about leftovers — they won't last long.

Coarse sugar adds a nice "frosty" look, but it isn't a necessity.

Use flaked or shredded coconut in place of coarse sugar.

Variation
Use your favorite flavor of cake. The white cake is easier to cover with frosting.

1	pkg (18.25 oz/515 g) cake mix, any flavor	1
22	round red- or green-and-white striped peppermint candies	22
1	container (15 oz/450 g) ready-to-serve frosting	1
	Coarse sugar, optional	
	Assorted candies to decorate (licorice mints, gumdrops, jelly beans, marshmallows, fruit leather)	

1. **Cake:** Prepare cake mix according to package directions. Spread in prepared pans, putting slightly more batter in the larger pan. Bake for 30 to 35 minutes or until a tester inserted in the center comes out clean. Cool 10 minutes, then remove from pans to a wire rack. Cool completely.

2. **Decoration:** Arrange round peppermint candies on foil-lined baking sheet to resemble a hat. Bake about 5 minutes or just until candies start to melt and stick together. Cool completely.

3. Place cake rounds on cake board with smaller one on top for the head. Cover entire cake with prepared frosting. Sprinkle coarse sugar over frosting. Put candy hat in place. Decorate rest of snowman as desired.

Ice Cream Cookies

Preheat oven to 375°F (190°C)
Baking sheets, greased

MAKES 15 SANDWICH COOKIES OR 30 SINGLE COOKIES

These yummy cookies are perfect for birthday parties, pool parties and after-school treats. Let children decorate their treat. You may need a few ice cream flavors, but the results will be worth it.

Tips
The cookies should be crisp for ice cream sandwiches. Bake cookies on middle oven rack. Turn baking sheet half way through baking to ensure even browning.

Let children enjoy making their own ice cream sandwich.

Variation
Replace candy-coated chocolate bits with mini chocolate chips.

1	pkg (18.25 oz/515 g) white cake mix	1
2	eggs	2
$\frac{1}{2}$ cup	butter, melted	125 mL
$1\frac{3}{4}$ cups	candy coated chocolate bits, divided	425 mL
2 qts	ice cream, any flavors, slightly softened	2 L

1. In a large mixer bowl, combine cake mix, eggs and melted butter. Beat on low speed for 1 minute or just until smooth. Stir in $1\frac{1}{4}$ cups (300 mL) of the candy coated chocolate bits. Mix well.

2. Drop dough by heaping spoonfuls onto prepared baking sheet 2 inches (5 cm) apart. Flatten slightly with floured fingers. Press 7 or 8 of the remaining candies into each cookie. Bake, one sheet at a time, for 10 to 14 minutes or until lightly browned. Cool 1 minute on baking sheet or until firm, then transfer cookies to racks and cool completely.

3. Sandwich two cookies with about $\frac{1}{2}$ cup (125 mL) of the ice cream between them. Press together lightly. Wrap well in plastic wrap. Freeze until firm, about 1 hours, or for up to 3 months.

Festive Coconut Fruitcake

Preheat oven to 300°F (150°C)
Three 8½ by 4½-inch (1.5 L) loaf pans, greased and
lined with greased brown paper or aluminum foil

MAKES ABOUT
60 SLICES

An abundance of colorful fruit, nuts and coconut gives this cake a festive air.

Tips
Place a shallow pan of hot water at the back of the oven during baking to keep this cake most.

If the top of the cake seems to be drying out during baking, cover it lightly with a double layer of ungreased brown paper or foil.

Fruitcake is easiest to slice when it's cold.

Variation
You can vary the kind of candied fruit and nuts in this cake as long as you keep the total amount the same.

2 cups	candied cherries, halved	500 mL
2 cups	mixed candied fruit	500 mL
1½ cups	light raisins	375 mL
1½ cups	slivered almonds	375 mL
1½ cups	flaked coconut	375 mL
1 cup	diced candied pineapple	250 mL
⅓ cup	all-purpose flour	75 mL
1	pkg (18.25 oz/515 g) white cake mix	1
1	pkg (4-serving size) vanilla instant pudding mix	1
3	eggs	3
⅓ cup	water	75 mL
⅓ cup	vegetable oil	75 mL
1 tsp	almond extract	5 mL

1. **Cake:** In a large bowl, stir together cherries, candied fruit, raisins, almonds, coconut, pineapple and flour. Mix well. Set aside. In a large mixer bowl, combine cake mix, pudding mix, eggs, water, oil and almond extract. Beat on medium speed for 2 minutes. Pour batter over fruit mixture. Mix well.

2. Spread batter evenly in prepared pans. Bake for 1½ hours or until a tester inserted in the center comes out clean. Cool 30 minutes in pans on a wire rack then remove from pans and cool completely on rack. (If you have covered the loaves with paper or foil during baking, remove before turning out onto rack.) Wrap in airtight plastic bags and store in the refrigerator for at least 1 week, or up to 6 months. Cut into serving-size slices.

Pumpkin Pie Squares

Preheat oven to 350°F (180°C)
13- by 9-inch (3 L) cake pan, greased

SERVES 12 TO 16

These tasty squares are similar in taste and texture to pumpkin pie but with a crunchy nut top.

Tips
If you buy nuts in bulk by weight, approximately 4 oz (125 g) of chopped nuts is 1 cup (250 mL).

Use a food processor to quickly mix the topping.

Variations
Replace white cake mix with a yellow one.

For an extra-rich filling, use whipping (35%) cream in place of the evaporated milk.

CRUST

1	pkg (18.25 oz/515 g) white cake mix, divided	1
½ cup	butter, softened	125 mL
1	egg	1

FILLING

3	eggs	3
1 cup	packed brown sugar	250 mL
3½ cups	pure pumpkin purée (not pie filling)	875 mL
½ cup	evaporated milk	125 mL
2½ tsp	ground cinnamon	12 mL
1 tsp	ground allspice	5 mL

TOPPING

⅓ cup	packed brown sugar	75 mL
½ tsp	ground cinnamon	2 mL
¼ cup	butter	50 mL
1 cup	chopped pecans	250 mL
	Whipped cream, optional	

1. **Crust:** Measure out 1 cup (250 mL) dry cake mix. Set aside. In a large mixer bowl, combine remaining cake mix, butter and egg. Beat on low speed for 1 minute or until crumbly. Press firmly into prepared pan.

2. **Filling:** In a large mixer bowl, combine eggs, brown sugar, pumpkin, evaporated milk, and spices. Beat on low speed to blend, then on medium speed until smooth. Pour over crust.

3. **Topping:** In a bowl, combine reserved cake mix, brown sugar and cinnamon. Cut in butter with pastry blender or two knives until crumbly. Stir in pecans. Sprinkle evenly over filling. Bake for 60 to 70 minutes or until set. Cool at least 30 minutes in pan on wire rack. Cut into squares and top with whipped cream, if desired. Store in refrigerator.

Colorful Christmas Cream Cake

Preheat oven to 350°F (180°C)
Three 9- by 5-inch (2 L) loaf pans, greased and
lined with greased aluminum foil

SERVES 12 TO 16

Layers of red,
white and green
cake under a
snowy white
cream cover make
for a colorful
conversation
piece that is also
delicious to eat.

Tips

If softened gelatin
sets too quickly, you
can reheat it and
try again.

Don't go overboard
with the food colors.
Pastel is pretty and
more appealing. Also,
the colors will darken
during baking.

Add food coloring
gradually, a few drops
at a time, until you
have reached the
desired shade.

CAKE

1	pkg (18.25 oz/515 g) white cake mix	1
3	eggs	3
1 1/3 cups	water	325 mL
1/3 cup	vegetable oil	75 mL
	Green and red food coloring	

FILLING & TOPPING

2 tsp	unflavored gelatin	10 mL
2 cups	whipping (35%) cream, divided	500 mL
3 tbsp	confectioner's (icing) sugar, sifted	45 mL
1/4 cup	raspberry or strawberry jam, divided	50 mL
3/4 cup	flaked coconut, divided	175 mL

1. **Crust:** In a large mixer bowl, combine cake mix, eggs, water and oil. Beat on medium speed for 2 minutes. Measure 1 2/3 cups (400 mL) of the batter into each of 2 separate bowls. Tint batter in first bowl light green with a few drops of coloring. Spread batter in a prepared pan. Tint batter in second bowl pink with a few drops of coloring. Spread batter in another pan. Spread remaining white batter in third pan. Bake for 20 to 25 minutes or until a tester inserted in the center comes out clean. Cool 10 minutes; remove from pans to wire racks. Remove foil and cool completely.

Tips

If you prefer more vibrant colors, look for paste food coloring in cake decorating supply stores.

To color coconut, put it in a plastic bag. Add a drop of food coloring and knead well.

Variations

Use different colors for other occasions, such as pink, red and white for Valentine's Day or pink, yellow and green for Easter.

Color the filling a pale red or green, if desired.

Decorate with candy canes or gumdrop Christmas trees.

2. ***Filling & Topping:*** Sprinkle gelatin over $\frac{1}{3}$ cup (75 mL) of the cream in small saucepan. Let stand for 10 minutes to soften. Then stir over low heat until gelatin is dissolved. Remove from heat. In a small mixer bowl, beat remaining cream and confectioner's sugar until frothy. Gradually add gelatin mixture, beating until stiff peaks form.

3. ***Assembly:*** Place green cake on platter. Spread half of the jam on top, then $\frac{1}{2}$ cup (125 mL) of the cream filling. Sprinkle with $\frac{1}{4}$ cup (50 mL) of the coconut. Repeat layering with white cake, jam, cream filling and coconut. Place pink cake layer on top. Cover top and sides of cake with remaining cream. Color remaining coconut pale green with 1 drop of food coloring. Sprinkle over cake. Chill at least 1 hour before slicing. Store leftover cake in the refrigerator.

Merry-Go-Round Magic

Preheat oven to 350°F (180°C)
10-inch (3 L) Bundt pan, greased and floured

SERVES 12

This carousel cake makes a great centerpiece for a children's birthday party.

Tips
A turntable makes a great cake plate for the carousel.

Use ready-made cookies or prepare your own using a sugar cookie recipe.

Variation
I love the chocolate cake but you can use any of your favorite flavors prepared in a Bundt pan.

CAKE

1	pkg (18.25 oz/515 g) devil's food cake mix	1
1	pkg (4-serving size) chocolate instant pudding mix	1
4	eggs	4
1 cup	sour cream	250 mL
½ cup	vegetable oil	125 mL
½ cup	water	125 mL
1 cup	semi-sweet chocolate chips, optional	250 mL

DECORATION

½ cup	ready-to-serve vanilla frosting	125 mL
	Food coloring, optional	
	Candy sprinkles, optional	
	Paper carousel roof (see directions, below)	
6	5-inch (12.5 cm) candy sticks	6
6	animal cookies	6

1. **Cake:** In a large mixer bowl, combine cake mix, pudding mix, eggs, sour cream, oil and water. Beat on low speed for 1 minute to blend, then on medium speed for 2 minutes. Stir in chocolate chips. Spread batter evenly in prepared pan. Bake for 50 to 60 minutes or until a tester inserted in the center comes out clean. Cool 25 minutes in pan on a wire rack, then remove from pan and cool completely on rack.

2. **Decoration:** Warm frosting for about 5 seconds in microwave. Tint pale green or pink, if desired. Spoon over cake to glaze. Decorate with sprinkles, if desired.

3. For roof, cut a 12-inch (30 cm) circle from colored paper. Scallop edge and decorate with crayons, if desired. Make 1 slit to center of circle. Overlap cut edges to form a peaked roof. Fasten in place with tape. Arrange candy sticks evenly around cake pressing in to secure. Lean cookie against each stick. Place roof on top.

Santa Claus Cupcakes

Preheat oven to 350°F (180°C)
Two 12-cup muffin tins, lined with paper liners

MAKES 24 CUPCAKES

These cupcakes are as much fun to make as they are to eat. Kids will love to help with the decorating for a holiday party.

Tip
Have extra candies on hand because the favorites will be eaten before they get to the cupcakes.

Variation
Don't limit the decorating to Santa faces. Try reindeer or other holiday favorites, such as snowmen, trees and bells.

1	pkg (18.25 oz/515 g) cake mix, any flavor	1
1	container (15 oz/450 g) ready-to-serve frosting	1
1/4 cup	red colored sprinkles or sugar	50 mL
48	semi-sweet chocolate chips	48
24	cinnamon candies	24
1 1/2 cups	miniature white marshmallows	375 mL

1. Prepare and bake cake mix according to package directions for cupcakes. Cool completely in pans on a wire rack.

2. Spread frosting over top of cupcakes. Sprinkle top 1/3 of each cupcake with red sprinkles to look like Santa's hat. Make face using chocolate chips for eyes and cinnamon candy for nose. Cut 12 marshmallows in half lengthwise and place under sprinkles to form the rim of Santa's hat. Cut 4 marshmallows in half crosswise. Place on lower part of cupcake to form beard.

Lemon Angel Torte *(page 106)* ►
Overleaf: Spicy Oatmeal Raisin Cookies *(page 134)*,
Lemon Crisps *(page 137)* and
Chocolate Caramel Pecan Cookies *(page 132)*

Chocolate Candy Cane Cake

Preheat oven to 350°F (180°C)
13- by 9-inch (3 L) cake pan, greased

MAKES 12 TO 16 SERVINGS

This holiday cake is simple to make but very festive.

Tip
Crush leftover candy canes and stir into vanilla ice cream.

Variation
Replace candy canes with hard mint candies to enjoy this cake year round.

CAKE

1	pkg (18.25 oz/515 g) devil's food cake mix	1
3	eggs	3
1⅓ cups	milk	325 mL
1 cup	mayonnaise	250 mL
1 tsp	peppermint extract	5 mL

FROSTING

1	container (15 oz/450 g) ready-to-serve buttercream frosting	1
¼ cup	crushed candy canes	50 mL
	Whole small candy canes to decorate	

1. **Cake:** In a large mixer bowl, combine cake mix, eggs, milk, mayonnaise and peppermint extract. Beat on medium speed for 2 minutes. Spread batter evenly in prepared pan. Bake for 35 to 40 minutes or until a tester inserted in the center comes out clean. Cool completely in pan on a wire rack.

2. Stir crushed candy canes into frosting. Spread frosting over top of cake. Decorate with whole candy canes.

Pumpkin 'n' Cream Cake

Preheat oven to 350°F (180°C)
13- by 9-inch (3 L) cake pan, greased

SERVES 12 TO 16

Even if you don't like pumpkin pie, you'll love this dessert.

Tips
Be sure to buy pumpkin purée, not pumpkin pie filling, which has sugar and spices added to it.

As eggs separate more easily when they are cold, it is best to separate eggs as soon as you remove them from the refrigerator. Let them come to room temperature before using. Even a trace of yolk in the whites will prevent them from beating into stiff peaks.

Variation
Change the kinds or amount of spice to suit your own taste.

CAKE

1	pkg (18.25 oz/515 g) white cake mix	1
1	pkg (4-serving size) vanilla instant pudding mix	1
2 cups	pumpkin purée	500 mL
3	eggs, separated	3
1/3 cup	water	75 mL
1/4 cup	rum	50 mL
1/4 cup	vegetable oil	50 mL
2 tsp	ground cinnamon	10 mL
1/2 tsp	ground nutmeg	2 mL
1/4 tsp	ground ginger	1 mL

TOPPING

1 1/2 cups	whipping (35%) cream	375 mL
1/4 cup	confectioner's (icing) sugar, sifted	50 mL
1 tbsp	rum	15 mL
1 oz	semi-sweet chocolate, melted, optional	30 g

1. **Cake:** In a large mixer bowl, combine cake mix, pudding mix, pumpkin, egg yolks, water, rum, oil and cinnamon, nutmeg and ginger. Beat on low speed for 1 minute to blend, then on medium speed for 2 minutes (batter will be thick). In another mixer bowl, beat egg whites to stiff peaks. Fold 1/4 of whites into pumpkin mixture thoroughly, then gently fold in remaining whites. Spread batter evenly in prepared pan. Bake for 30 to 35 minutes or until a tester inserted in the center comes out clean. Cool completely in pan on a wire rack.

2. **Topping:** Beat whipping cream and confectioner's sugar to soft peaks. Add rum; beat to stiff peaks. Spread over cake. Decorate top with a drizzle of melted chocolate, if desired.

Cookies

Chocolate Caramel Pecan Cookies

Preheat oven to 375°F (190°C)
Baking sheets, greased

1	pkg (18.25 oz/515 g) white cake mix	1
2	eggs	2
½ cup	butter, melted	125 mL
6 oz	semi-sweet chocolate, chopped	175 g
25	individual soft caramels, quartered	25
¾ cup	chopped pecans	175 mL

Tips
Place cookies
2 inches (5 cm) apart
to allow for spreading
during baking.

Bake cookies, one
tray at a time, on
middle oven rack.

If baking sheets are
warm, let them cool
before putting dough
on them.

Variation
Replace white cake
mix with yellow.

1. In a large mixer bowl, combine cake mix, eggs and melted butter. Beat on low speed for 1 minute or just until smooth. Stir in chocolate, caramels and pecans. Mix well.

2. Drop dough by rounded tablespoonfuls (15 mL) onto prepared baking sheets 2 inches (5 cm) apart. Flatten slightly with fingers. Bake, one sheet at a time, for 8 to 12 minutes or until lightly browned. Cool 1 minute on baking sheets or until firm, then transfer cookies to wire racks and cool completely.

Crispy Chocolate Chunk Cookies

Preheat oven to 375°F (190°C)
Baking sheets, greased

**MAKES ABOUT
4 DOZEN COOKIES**

The addition of crispy rice cereal gives these cookies a pleasingly chewy texture that compliments the chocolate.

1	pkg (18.25 oz/515 g) devil's food cake mix	1
2	eggs	2
½ cup	butter, melted	125 mL
6 oz	semi-sweet chocolate, coarsely chopped	175 g
1½ cups	crisp rice cereal	375 mL

1. In a large mixer bowl, combine cake mix, eggs and melted butter. Beat on low speed for 1 minute or just until smooth. Stir in chocolate and cereal. Mix well.

2. Drop dough by rounded tablespoonfuls (15 mL) onto prepared baking sheets 2 inches (5 cm) apart. Flatten slightly with fingers. Bake, one sheet at a time, for 8 to 12 minutes or until set. Cool 1 minute on baking sheets or until firm, then transfer cookies to racks and cool completely.

Tips

Shiny aluminium baking sheets produce cookies that are evenly browned and crisp on the bottom, which also improves the flavor. Insulated pans prevent browning, producing a softer cookie.

To ensure even browning, turn sheet back to front halfway through baking.

Variation

Replace chocolate cake mix with white.

Spicy Oatmeal Raisin Cookies

Preheat oven to 375°F (190°C)
Baking sheets, greased

MAKES ABOUT
4 DOZEN COOKIES

Once a favorite,
always a favorite.

Tips
Use quick-cooking oats to make cookies. You can use large-flake for a more "oaty" taste but the texture will change slightly.

Don't let cookies remain on the baking sheet longer than 1 minute. They will continue to cook and be more difficult to remove.

Variation
Replace raisins with dried cranberries or a mixture of other dried fruits such as papaya, pineapple, mango and dates. Adjust spice to suit your own tastes.

1	pkg (18.25 oz/515 g) white cake mix	1
1 cup	quick-cooking oats	250 mL
2 tsp	ground cinnamon	10 mL
1 tsp	ground nutmeg	5 mL
2	eggs	2
$\frac{1}{2}$ cup	vegetable oil	125 mL
1 cup	raisins	250 mL

1. In a large mixer bowl, combine cake mix, oats, cinnamon, nutmeg, eggs and oil. Beat on low speed for 1 minute or just until blended. Stir in raisins. Mix well.

2. Drop dough by rounded tablespoonfuls (15 mL) onto prepared baking sheets 2 inches (5 cm) apart. Flatten slightly with fingers. Bake, one sheet at a time, for 8 to 12 minutes or until lightly browned. Cool 1 minute on baking sheets or until firm, then transfer cookies to wire racks and cool completely.

Refrigerator Nut Wafers

Preheat oven to 375°F (190°C)
Baking sheets, greased

**MAKES ABOUT
7 DOZEN COOKIES**

*With a roll of
dough in the
refrigerator,
fresh baked
cookies are only
minutes away.*

Tips
You can make square
cookies by packing
dough into small
plastic wrap boxes.

Roll dough in finely
chopped nuts before
slicing for an
attractive edge
around the cookie.

Variation
Try pistachio nuts for
an unusual look. The
green is especially
pretty at Christmas.

1	pkg (18.25 oz/515 g) white cake mix	1
1	egg	1
½ cup	butter, melted	125 mL
1 tbsp	water	15 mL
1 tsp	vanilla	5 mL
1½ cups	chopped pecans or hazelnuts	375 mL

1. In a large mixer bowl, combine cake mix, egg, melted butter, water and vanilla. Stir with wooden spoon to blend. Work in nuts with your hands to form smooth dough.

2. Divide dough in half. Shape each half into a 2-inch (5 cm) thick log. Wrap in plastic wrap or waxed paper and chill overnight in refrigerator. Cut dough into ⅛-inch (3 mm) thick slices. Place on prepared baking sheets 2 inches (5 cm) apart. Bake, one sheet at a time, for 7 to 9 minutes or until lightly browned. Cool 1 minute on baking sheets or until firm, then transfer cookies to racks and cool completely.

Cereal Crisps

Preheat oven to 375°F (190°C)
Baking sheets, greased

**MAKES ABOUT
4 DOZEN COOKIES**

*Cereal never
tasted so good.
There's a lot of
crunch packed
into every bite. It
won't be hard to
convince kids to
eat breakfast.*

Tips
Measure cereal then
crush it slightly. If
you crush then
measure, you will
have too much.

Cookies bake
quickly. Always
check them at the
minimum time, and
then watch carefully.
It's always wise to
slightly underbake
rather than overbake
cookies. This means
you'll have a slightly
chewy cookie, which
is preferable to
hard rocks!

Variation
Omit nuts if allergies
are a problem.

1	pkg (18.25 oz/515 g) white cake mix	1
1	egg	1
½ cup	water	125 mL
½ cup	vegetable oil	125 mL
1¼ cups	crisp rice cereal	300 mL
¾ cup	corn flakes cereal	175 mL
½ cup	flaked coconut	125 mL
½ cup	chopped walnuts	125 mL

1. In a large mixer bowl, combine cake mix, egg, water and oil. Beat on low speed for 1 minute or until blended. Stir in cereals, coconut and nuts. Mix well.

2. Drop dough by rounded tablespoonfuls (15 mL) onto prepared baking sheets 2 inches (5 cm) apart. Bake, one sheet at a time, for 9 to 11 minutes or until lightly browned. Cool 1 minute on baking sheets or until firm, then transfer cookies to racks and cool completely.

Lemon Crisps

Preheat oven to 350°F (180°C)
Baking sheets, greased

MAKES ABOUT
4 DOZEN COOKIES

Crisp and lemony — a wonderful plain cookie to enjoy with a cup of tea.

Tips
When grating the zest from lemons and oranges, use only the colored part. The white underneath has a bitter flavor.

You can mix the dough easily with an electric mixer on low speed for 1 minute.

Variation
Make these into sandwich cookies by putting 2 cookies together with a lemon frosting or raspberry jam.

1	pkg (18.25 oz/515 g) lemon cake mix	1
1	egg	1
½ cup	butter, melted	125 mL
1 tsp	grated lemon zest	5 mL
	Granulated sugar	

1. In a large mixer bowl, combine cake mix, egg, melted butter and lemon zest. Mix with wooden spoon until well blended.

2. Shape dough into 1-inch (2.5 cm) balls. Roll in granulated sugar. Place on prepared baking sheets 2 inches (5 cm) apart. Press flat with bottom of a glass dipped in sugar. Bake, one tray at a time, for 10 to 12 minutes or until lightly browned around edges. Cool 1 minute on baking sheets or until firm, then transfer cookies to wire racks and cool completely.

Almond Crisps

Preheat oven to 375°F (190°C)
Baking sheets, greased

MAKES ABOUT
4 DOZEN COOKIES

A plain crisp cookie with a delightful almond flavor.

Tips
Use unblanched almonds for an attractive appearance. The flecks of brown skin add a nice flavor, too.

Cooled cookies can be frozen in airtight plastic bags for up to 6 months.

Variation
Replace almonds with hazelnuts or pecans. Replace almond extract with vanilla.

1	pkg (18.25 oz/515 g) white cake mix	1
1 cup	very finely chopped or ground almonds	250 mL
1	egg	1
1/2 cup	butter, melted	125 mL
1 tbsp	water	15 mL
1 tsp	almond extract	5 mL
	Granulated sugar	
	Whole almonds, optional	

1. In a large mixer bowl, combine cake mix, almonds, egg, melted butter, water and almond extract. Mix with wooden spoon or on low speed of mixer until blended, about 1 minute.

2. Shape dough into 1-inch (2.5 cm) balls. Place on prepared baking sheets 2 inches (5 cm) apart. Press flat with bottom of glass dipped in sugar. If desired, press an almond on top of each cookie. Bake, one sheet at a time, for 10 to 12 minutes or until lightly browned. Cool 1 minute on baking sheets or until firm, then transfer cookies to wire racks and cool completely.

Chocolate Peanut Butter Cookies

Preheat oven to 350°F (180°C)
Baking sheets, greased

MAKES ABOUT 3½ DOZEN COOKIES

These cookies are just like peanuts — you can't stop at just one.

Tips
Use creamy peanut butter for easy blending. You can always add chopped peanuts for the crunch.

The best baking sheets for cookies have little or no sides. This allows the heat to circulate during baking, resulting in even browning.

Variation
For chocolate lovers, use chocolate chips or chocolate-covered peanuts.

1	pkg (18.25 oz/515 g) devil's food cake mix	1
1 cup	creamy peanut butter	250 mL
2	eggs	2
¼ cup	milk	50 mL
1 cup	peanut butter chips	250 mL
¾ cup	chopped peanuts	175 mL

1. In a large mixer bowl, combine cake mix, peanut butter, eggs and milk. Mix with wooden spoon or on low speed of mixer for 1 minute or until blended. Stir in chips and peanuts. Mix well.

2. Drop dough by rounded tablespoonfuls (15 mL) onto prepared baking sheets 2 inches (5 cm) apart. Bake, one sheet at a time, for 10 to 12 minutes, or until lightly browned. Cool 1 minute on baking sheets or until firm, then transfer cookies to wire racks and cool completely.

Crunchy Chocolate Dreams

Preheat oven to 375°F (190°C)
Baking sheets, greased

MAKES ABOUT
4 DOZEN COOKIES

The taste of
these rich, dark
cookies resembles
a chocolate bar.

Tips
A small ice cream
scoop with wire
release is ideal for
spooning out cookie
dough. It gives nicely
shaped cookies of
uniform size.

Line baking sheets
with parchment
paper or special
baking liners for easy
removal and cleanup.
This is especially
handy for cookies
that tend to stick.

Variations
Use yellow cake
mix for a traditional
chocolate chip
cookie look.

Replace nuts with
1 cup (250 mL)
flaked coconut or
dried fruit.

1	pkg (18.25 oz/515 g) devil's food cake mix	1
2	eggs	2
1/2 cup	vegetable oil	125 mL
1 cup	semi-sweet chocolate chips	250 mL
3/4 cup	chopped nuts	175 mL
3/4 cup	crunchy toffee bits	175 mL

1. In a large mixer bowl, combine cake mix, eggs and oil. With a wooden spoon or on low speed of mixer, mix for 1 minute or until well blended. Dough will be stiff. Stir in chocolate, nuts and toffee bits.

2. Drop dough by rounded tablespoonfuls (15 mL) onto prepared baking sheets 2 inches (5 cm) apart. Bake, one sheet at a time, for 8 to 12 minutes or until firm around the edges. Cool 1 minute on baking sheets, then transfer cookies to a wire rack and cool completely.

Hazelnut Biscotti

Preheat oven to 350°F (180°C)
Baking sheets, lined with parchment paper or greased

MAKES ABOUT
3 1/2 DOZEN COOKIES

A double baking makes biscotti extra crunchy so they are ideal to dunk into your favorite drink. They are also a good choice if you want to ship or mail a homemade gift.

Tips
When shaping the dough into rectangles, keep in mind that it will expand during baking so start slightly smaller than you prefer.

Parchment paper makes it easy to remove the baked rectangle.

Store biscotti in airtight containers for up to 3 weeks.

Variations
Use your favorite nut. Pecans and almonds are popular.

Omit lemon zest, if desired.

1	pkg (18.25 oz/515 g) white cake mix	1
2/3 cup	all-purpose flour	150 mL
1/3 cup	ground hazelnuts	75 mL
2	eggs	2
1/2 cup	vegetable oil	125 mL
1 tbsp	grated lemon zest	15 mL
2/3 cup	coarsely chopped hazelnuts	150 mL

1. In a large mixer bowl, combine cake mix, flour, ground hazelnuts, eggs, oil and zest. Beat on low speed for 1 minute or until blended. Work in chopped hazelnuts with hands to form smooth dough. Divide dough in half.

2. On a prepared baking sheet, shape each half into a 10- by 3-inch (25 by 8 cm) rectangle that is 1/2-inch (1 cm) deep. Bake, one sheet at a time, for 15 minutes. Remove from oven and cool 10 minutes on baking sheet. Carefully transfer to cutting board and cut each rectangle into 1/2-inch (1 cm) slices. Place slices on their side on baking sheets. Bake, one tray at a time, for 10 minutes. Turn slices over and bake for 5 to 10 minutes longer or until crisp and golden. Cool 1 minute on baking sheet, then transfer biscotti to wire racks and cool completely.

141

Toffee Almond Chocolate Chip Cookies

Preheat oven to 375°F (190°C)
Baking sheets, greased

MAKES ABOUT
3 ½ DOZEN COOKIES

Crunchy toffee bits, almonds and chocolate chips make these cookies a certain favorite.

1	pkg (18.25 oz/515 g) white cake mix	1
2	eggs	2
½ cup	butter, melted	125 mL
1 tsp	vanilla	5 mL
1 cup	chopped almonds	250 mL
¾ cup	crunchy toffee bits	175 mL
¾ cup	milk chocolate chips	175 mL

Tips
Bake cookies, one tray at a time, on middle oven rack.

For even browning, turn cookie sheet back to front halfway through baking.

To easily remove cookies, line sheets with parchment paper.

Bake less time for chewy cookies and more time for crisp cookies.

Variation
Replace almonds with pecans and milk chocolate chips with semi-sweet or white chips.

1. In a large mixer bowl, combine cake mix, eggs, melted butter and vanilla. Beat on low speed for 1 minute or just until smooth. Stir in almonds, toffee bits and chocolate chips. Mix well.

2. Drop dough by rounded tablespoonfuls (15 mL) onto prepared baking sheets 2 inches (5 cm) apart. Flatten slightly with fingers. Bake, one sheet at a time, for 10 to 12 minutes or until lightly browned. Cool 1 minute on baking sheets or until firm, then transfer cookies to wire racks and cool completely.

Bars & Squares

Toffee Chocolate Bars

Preheat oven to 350°F (180°C)
13- by 9-inch (3 L) cake pan, greased

**MAKES ABOUT
4 DOZEN BARS**

*Layers of
crunchy toffee
bits, creamy
caramel and
chocolate cover
a crisp cookie-like
base, making every
bite a sensation.*

Tips
The toffee bits
get softer if you
freeze these bars.
We love them both
ways, frozen and
soft or unfrozen
and crunchy. Take
your pick.

Don't leave the
filling unattended
on the stove – even
for a minute. It
burns very quickly.

Variation
Use milk chocolate
chips in place of
semi-sweet, if
you prefer.

CRUST

1	pkg (18.25 oz/515 g) white cake mix	1
2 tbsp	packed brown sugar	25 mL
1/2 cup	butter, melted	125 mL

FILLING

1	can (10 oz/300 mL) sweetened condensed milk	1
2 tbsp	butter	25 mL

TOPPING

1 2/3 cups	semi-sweet chocolate chips	400 mL
1 cup	crunchy toffee bits	250 mL

1. **Crust:** In a large bowl, combine cake mix, brown sugar and melted butter. Using a wooden spoon, mix until a soft dough forms. Press firmly into prepared pan. Bake for 15 minutes or until light golden. Cool slightly in pan on a wire rack.

2. **Filling:** Meanwhile, heat sweetened condensed milk and butter in a heavy saucepan, stirring constantly over low heat for 5 to 10 minutes or until thickened. Spread over crust. Bake for 10 to 15 minutes or until golden. Cool 1 hour in pan on a wire rack.

3. **Topping:** In a saucepan, over low heat (or in microwave on medium for 2 minutes), melt chocolate chips, stirring until smooth. Spread evenly over filling. Sprinkle toffee bits on top, pressing lightly into chocolate. Cool completely. If necessary, chill briefly to set chocolate. Cut into bars.

Chocolate Pecan Bars

Preheat oven to 350°F (180°C)
17- by 11-inch (45 by 28 cm) jellyroll pan, greased

MAKES ABOUT
5 DOZEN BARS

One pan goes a long way, so this recipe is a good choice for gift giving.

Tips
If you don't do much baking, shop at bulk stores for specialty items and smaller quantities. Remember to store nuts in the freezer.

Purchase good quality shiny metal pans for baking. They bake evenly and don't rust. If using glass pans or dark metal decrease your oven temperature by 25°F (10°C).

Variation
For better storage, omit the drizzle.

CRUST

1	pkg (18.25 oz/515 g) white cake mix	1
²⁄₃ cup	butter, melted	150 mL

TOPPING

5 oz	semi-sweet chocolate, chopped	150 g
1 cup	corn syrup	250 mL
1 cup	granulated sugar	250 mL
3	eggs	3
1 tsp	vanilla	5 mL
2¹⁄₂ cups	chopped pecans	625 mL

DRIZZLE, OPTIONAL

2 oz	semi-sweet chocolate, melted	60 g

1. **Crust:** In a large bowl, combine cake mix and melted butter. Using a wooden spoon, mix until a soft dough forms. Press firmly into prepared pan. Bake for 10 to 12 minutes or until light golden.

2. **Topping:** In a saucepan over low heat, heat chocolate and corn syrup, stirring until chocolate is melted and smooth. Remove from heat. Stir in sugar, eggs and vanilla until blended. Stir in pecans. Pour filling over warm crust; spread evenly. Bake for 30 to 35 minutes or until filling is set around edges and slightly soft in center. Cool completely in pan on a wire rack.

3. **Drizzle:** If desired, drizzle melted chocolate randomly over bars. Chill just to set chocolate. Cut into bars.

Chewy Coconut Nut Bars

Preheat oven to 350°F (180°C)
13- by 9-inch (3 L) cake pan, greased

MAKES ABOUT
4 DOZEN BARS

These are quick to make and a treat to eat.

Tips
I prefer flaked or shredded coconut. Desiccated coconut is very fine and results in drier baked products.

If you like a topping that is less sweet, add 1 tbsp (15 mL) lemon juice.

Variation
Pecans or walnuts work well in this recipe.

CRUST

1	pkg (18.25 oz/515 g) white cake mix	1
½ cup	butter, melted	125 mL

TOPPING

4	eggs	4
1¾ cups	packed brown sugar	425 mL
¼ cup	all-purpose flour	50 mL
2 tsp	baking powder	10 mL
1 tsp	vanilla	5 mL
1½ cups	chopped nuts	375 mL
1 cup	flaked coconut	250 mL

1. **Crust:** In a large bowl, combine cake mix and melted butter. Using a wooden spoon, mix until a soft dough forms. Press firmly into prepared pan. Bake for 15 minutes or until light golden.

2. **Topping:** In a bowl, beat eggs and brown sugar until blended. Stir in flour, baking powder and vanilla. Stir in nuts and coconut. Spread over warm crust. Bake for 25 to 30 minutes or until set and golden. Cool completely in pan on a wire rack. Cut into bars.

Candy Bar Bars

Preheat oven to 350°F (180°C)
13- by 9-inch (3 L) cake pan, greased

MAKES ABOUT
4 DOZEN BARS

The name says it all. These tasty bars are just like a candy bar.

Tip
There are several brands of soft caramels. Choose ones that are easy to unwrap, unless you have kids to do that for you.

Variation
Peanuts or a combination of peanuts and pecans also work well in this bar.

CRUST

1	pkg (18.25 oz/515 g) white cake mix	1
¾ cup	butter, melted	175 mL

FILLING

14 oz	soft caramels (about 50)	425 g
⅓ cup	evaporated milk	75 mL
⅓ cup	butter	75 mL
1⅔ cups	confectioner's (icing) sugar, sifted	400 mL
1 cup	chopped pecans	250 mL

GLAZE

1 cup	semi-sweet chocolate chips, melted	250 mL

1. **Crust:** In a bowl, combine cake mix and melted butter. Using a wooden spoon, mix until a soft dough forms. Press firmly into prepared pan. Bake for 15 to 20 minutes or until light golden.

2. **Filling:** In a saucepan, over low heat, heat caramels and evaporated milk, stirring often until smooth. Add butter, then stir until melted. Remove from heat. Stir in confectioner's sugar and pecans. Mix well. Spread over crust. Let cool until set.

3. **Glaze:** Spread melted chocolate over filling. Chill just to set chocolate. Cut into bars.

Cherry Cheesecake Bars

Preheat oven to 350°F (180°C)
13- by 9-inch (3 L) cake pan, greased

**MAKES ABOUT
3 DOZEN BARS**

Enjoy these bite-size cheesecakes for dessert or a snack. Vary the flavor to suit your family.

Tip
Melt butter in a measuring cup for easy drizzling.

Variation
Use any flavor of pie filling. Peach and blueberry are both delicious.

CRUST

1	pkg (18.25 oz/515 g) white cake mix, divided	1
½ cup	corn flake crumbs	125 mL
1	egg	1
½ cup	butter, melted	125 mL

FILLING

1 lb	cream cheese, softened	500 g
⅓ cup	granulated sugar	75 mL
2	eggs	2
1 tsp	grated lemon zest	5 mL
1 tbsp	lemon juice	15 mL
1	can (19 oz/540 mL) cherry pie filling	1

TOPPING

½ cup	chopped pecans	125 mL
½ tsp	ground cinnamon	2 mL
¼ cup	butter, melted	50 mL

1. **Crust:** Reserve ½ cup (125 mL) cake mix for topping. In a large bowl, combine remaining mix, corn flake crumbs, egg and butter. Using a wooden spoon, mix until a soft dough forms. Press firmly into bottom and slightly up sides of prepared pan. Chill while preparing filling.

2. **Filling:** In a large mixer bowl, beat cream cheese and sugar until blended. Add eggs, one at a time, beating thoroughly after each addition. Stir in lemon zest and juice. Spread over crust. Dollop tablespoonfuls of pie filling over cheese mixture.

3. **Topping:** In a bowl, combine reserved cake mix, pecans and cinnamon. Sprinkle over filling. Drizzle with melted butter. Bake for 40 to 50 minutes or just until set. Cool completely in pan on a wire rack. Refrigerate until serving. Cut into bars. Store leftover bars in the refrigerator.

Chocolate Caramel Pecan Crumble Bars

Preheat oven to 350°F (180°C)
13- by 9-inch (3 L) cake pan, greased

**MAKES ABOUT
3 DOZEN BARS**

*Easy to make and
delicious to eat!
These bars are an
excellent choice
to keep on hand
in the freezer.*

Tips
Chill caramels to
make unwrapping
a little easier. Slit
wrapper with a small
sharp knife to start.

Break up any
large lumps in
crumble mixture
with your fingers.

Variation
Use your favorite
nut in place of the
pecans. Walnuts,
hazelnuts, cashews
and almonds all
work well.

CRUST

1	pkg (18.25 oz/ 515 g) devil's food cake mix	1
1 cup	chopped pecans	250 mL
¾ cup	quick-cooking oats	175 mL
¾ cup	butter, melted	175 mL

TOPPING

1	can (10 oz/300 mL) sweetened condensed milk	1
7 oz	soft caramels (about 25 caramels)	210 g
¼ cup	butter	50 mL

1. **Crust:** In a large bowl, combine cake mix, pecans, oats and melted butter. Using a wooden spoon, mix until a soft dough forms. Reserve 1⅓ cups (325 mL) for topping. Press remainder in prepared pan. Bake for 15 minutes or until light golden.

2. **Topping:** In a heavy saucepan, over low heat, heat sweetened condensed milk, caramels and butter, stirring constantly until melted and smooth. Pour over warm crust. Sprinkle reserved crumble mixture evenly on top. Bake for 20 to 25 minutes longer or until golden and bubbly. Cool completely in pan on a wire rack. Cut into bars.

Raspberry Meringue Bars

Preheat oven to 350°F (180°C)
13- by 9-inch (3 L) cake pan, greased

**MAKES ABOUT
3 DOZEN BARS**

*A chewy meringue
topping with
lots of nuts and
coconut covers
a layer of jam
on a shortbread-
like base.*

Tips
Before beating
egg whites, wipe
the bowl with the
cut surface of a
lemon to make sure
it is free of grease.

Cut bars with a hot,
damp knife.

Variation
Try other flavors
of jam and nuts,
such as apricot jam
with hazelnuts.

CRUST

1	pkg (18.25 oz/515 g) white cake mix	1
½ cup	butter, melted	125 mL
2	egg yolks	2

TOPPING

1 cup	raspberry jam	250 mL
½ cup	flaked coconut	125 mL
2	egg whites	2
½ cup	granulated sugar	125 mL
1 cup	chopped walnuts	250 mL

1. ***Crust:*** In a large mixer bowl, combine cake mix, melted butter and egg yolks. Beat on low speed for about 1 minute until well blended. Press firmly in prepared pan. Bake for 12 to 15 minutes or until very lightly browned.

2. ***Topping:*** Spread jam over warm crust. Sprinkle coconut on top. In a small mixer bowl, beat egg whites until frothy. Gradually add sugar, beating until stiff peaks form. Fold in walnuts. Carefully spread over coconut. Bake for 20 to 25 minutes or until light golden. Cool completely in pan on a wire rack. Cut into bars.

Pecan Toffee Bars

Preheat oven to 350°F (180°C)
13- by 9-inch (3 L) cake pan, greased

MAKES ABOUT
3 DOZEN BARS

This easy-to-make treat is quite sweet and very popular.

Tips
Cut cooled bars and pack them in a single layer to freeze. If the bars are cut when they are frozen, you can thaw at any time just the number you want to serve.

A drizzle of melted chocolate makes these bars special. If they have been frozen, add the drizzle just before serving.

Variation
Replace toffee bits with chopped toffee-crunch chocolate bars.

CRUST

1	pkg (18.25 oz/515 g) white cake mix	1
1/2 cup	butter, melted	125 mL
1	egg	1

TOPPING

1	can (10 oz/300 mL) sweetened condensed milk	1
1	egg	1
1 1/4 cups	chopped pecans	300 mL
1 1/3 cups	crunchy toffee bits	325 mL

1. **Crust:** In a large mixer bowl, combine cake mix, melted butter and egg. Beat on low speed for about 1 minute until crumbly. Press firmly in prepared pan. Bake for 15 to 20 minutes or until light golden.

2. **Topping:** In a bowl, combine sweetened condensed milk and egg. Mix well. Stir in pecans and toffee bits. Pour evenly over crust. Bake for 25 to 30 minutes or until set. Cool completely in pan on a wire rack. Cut into bars.

Chewy Peanut Candy Squares

Preheat oven to 350°F (180°C)
15- by 10-inch (38 by 25 cm) jellyroll pan, greased

MAKES ABOUT
4 DOZEN BARS

These chewy treats are always a big hit with kids, young and old.

Tip
Buy peanut butter just as you need it to retain the fresh taste in baked goods.

Variation
Colored marshmallows are a fun choice.

CRUST

1	pkg (18.25 oz/515 g) white cake mix	1
¹⁄₂ cup	butter, softened	125 mL
1	egg	1

TOPPING

3¹⁄₂ cups	miniature marshmallows	825 mL
³⁄₄ cup	corn syrup	175 mL
³⁄₄ cup	packed brown sugar	175 mL
³⁄₄ cup	creamy peanut butter	175 mL
2 cups	crisp rice cereal	500 mL
1³⁄₄ cups	salted peanuts	425 mL
1¹⁄₄ cups	miniature candy coated chocolate candy	300 mL

1. **Crust:** In a large mixer bowl, combine cake mix, butter and egg. Beat on low speed for 1 minute until crumbly. Press firmly in prepared pan. Bake for 10 to 15 minutes or until light golden.

2. **Topping:** Sprinkle marshmallows over hot crust. Return to oven for 1 to 2 minutes or just until marshmallows begin to puff. Cool slightly in pan on a wire rack.

3. In a large saucepan, combine syrup, brown sugar and peanut butter. Heat over low heat, stirring constantly, until smooth. Remove from heat. Stir in cereal, peanuts and candy. Spread evenly over marshmallows. Cool completely before cutting into squares.

Desserts

Butterscotch Fudge Torte

Preheat oven to 350°F (180°C)
10-inch (25 cm) springform pan

SERVES 12 TO 16

No matter how it's presented, the combination of butterscotch, chocolate and nuts is a favorite.

Tips
Prepare this a day ahead and leave more time for last-minute dinner preparations.

Heat the butterscotch mixture in a microwave on medium power for about 1 minute.

The applesauce should be unsweetened because there's enough sugar in the cake.

Variation
Replace butterscotch with semi-sweet chocolate chips.

⅔ cup	butterscotch chips	150 mL
½ cup	sweetened condensed milk	125 mL
1	pkg (18.25 oz/515 g) devil's food cake mix	1
½ cup	butter, melted, divided	125 mL
2	eggs	2
1 cup	unsweetened applesauce	250 mL
⅔ cup	coarsely chopped cashews	150 mL

1. In a small saucepan, over low heat, heat butterscotch chips and sweetened condensed milk, stirring often until melted and smooth. Set aside.

2. In a large mixer bowl, combine cake mix and ⅓ cup (75 mL) of the melted butter. Beat on low speed until crumbly. Reserve 1 cup (250 mL) of mixture for topping. Add eggs and applesauce to remaining cake mixture. Beat on low speed for 1 minute to blend, then on medium speed for 3 minutes. Spread batter evenly in prepared pan. Drizzle butterscotch mixture over batter. Stir cashews and remaining melted butter into reserved cake mixture. Mix well. Sprinkle over cake. Bake for 45 to 50 minutes or until set. Cool 20 minutes on a wire rack then remove from pan and cool completely on rack.

Strawberry Lime Cream Squares

Preheat oven to 350°F (180°C)
13- by 9-inch (3 L) cake pan, greased

SERVES 12 TO 16

This refreshingly light fruit dessert will remind you of summer any time of the year.

Tip
Store leftover egg whites in a covered container in the refrigerator for up to 4 days.

Variation
Use any of your favorite berries in this recipe. Raspberries, blueberries or a combination are all good.

CRUST

1	pkg (18.25 oz/515 g) white cake mix	1
1/2 cup	finely chopped pecans	125 mL
1/2 cup	butter, melted	125 mL

FILLING

1	can (10 oz/300 mL) sweetened condensed milk	1
3	egg yolks	3
1 tbsp	grated lime zest	15 mL
2/3 cup	fresh lime juice	150 mL
1	drop green food coloring, optional	1

TOPPING

3 cups	sliced fresh strawberries	750 mL
8 oz	frozen whipped topping, thawed	1 L

1. **Crust:** In a large bowl, combine cake mix, pecans and melted butter. Using a wooden spoon, mix until a soft dough forms. Press firmly into prepared pan. Bake for 10 minutes or until golden.

2. **Filling:** In a small bowl, combine sweetened condensed milk, egg yolks, lime zest, juice and coloring, stirring until smooth. Pour evenly over crust. Bake for about 15 minutes or until set. Cool 15 minutes in pan on a wire rack, then refrigerate until cold, about 30 minutes. Scatter berries over filling. Spread whipped topping over fruit. Chill until serving. Store leftover dessert in the refrigerator.

Super Simple Rhubarb Dessert

Preheat oven to 350°F (180°C)
13- by 9-inch (3 L) cake pan, greased

SERVES 12 TO 16

Welcome spring by enjoying the refreshing flavor of fresh rhubarb in this delicious dessert.

Tips

If using frozen rhubarb, thaw and pat well to dry before using.

The rhubarb sinks, forming a tart creamy fruit mixture under a tender, light layer of cake.

Variations

Replace 2 cups (500 mL) of the rhubarb with fresh strawberries or raspberries.

Replace cinnamon with ground ginger or grated orange zest.

1	pkg (18.25 oz/515 g) white cake mix	1
3	eggs	3
1⅓ cups	water	325 mL
⅓ cup	vegetable oil	75 mL
1 tsp	ground cinnamon	5 mL
6 cups	fresh or frozen rhubarb	1.5 L
1 cup	granulated sugar	250 mL
1 cup	whipping (35%) cream	250 mL

1. In a large mixer bowl, combine cake mix, eggs, water, oil and cinnamon. Beat on medium speed for 2 minutes. Spread batter evenly in prepared pan. Sprinkle rhubarb evenly over batter. Sprinkle sugar over rhubarb and drizzle cream on top. Do not mix. Bake for 35 to 40 minutes or until set. Cool in pan on a wire rack. Serve warm or cold. Store in refrigerator.

Plum Küchen

Preheat oven to 400°F (200°C)
13- by 9-inch (3 L) cake pan, greased

Tip
Red plums are colorful, but the black ones are tasty, too.

Variations
Replace plums with nectarines.

Use a yellow cake mix in place of the white.

CAKE

1	pkg (18.25 oz/515 g) white cake mix	1
¾ cup	butter	175 mL
2	eggs	2
⅓ cup	milk	75 mL
6	large, fresh plums, pitted and cut into eighths	6
1 cup	seedless grapes, green or red	250 mL

TOPPING

¼ cup	butter, melted	50 mL
¼ cup	granulated sugar	50 mL
1 tsp	ground cinnamon	5 mL

1. ***Cake:*** In a large bowl, cut butter into cake mix with pastry blender or 2 knives until mixture resembles coarse crumbs. Add eggs and milk, stirring until smooth, about 1 minute. Spread evenly in prepared pan. Arrange plum slices in 3 lengthwise rows over batter. Place grapes between rows.

2. ***Topping:*** In a small bowl, combine melted butter, sugar and cinnamon. Mix until well blended. Spoon evenly over fruit. Bake for 30 to 40 minutes or until set and fruit is tender. Cool in pan on a wire rack for 30 minutes. Enjoy warm with ice cream or whipped cream.

Mango Mousse Cake

Preheat oven to 350°F (180°C)
Two 9-inch (23 cm) round cake pans, greased and floured
9-inch (23 cm) springform pan

SERVES 12 TO 16

Refreshingly light but creamy, this is a memorable dessert to complete a special dinner.

Tips
Use ripe mangos for the mousse but slightly firmer ones to garnish.

Brush mango slices lightly with lemon juice to keep them fresh.

Prepare the day before to let mousse set.

Variation
This dessert is also outstanding using a chocolate cake mix.

CAKE

1	pkg (18.25 oz/515 g) white cake mix	1
3	eggs	3
1 tbsp	grated orange zest	15 mL
1$\frac{2}{3}$ cups	orange juice	400 mL
$\frac{1}{3}$ cup	vegetable oil	75 mL

MANGO MOUSSE

1	envelope ($\frac{1}{4}$ oz/7 g or 1 tbsp/15 mL) unflavored gelatin	1
$\frac{1}{4}$ cup	orange liqueur	50 mL
2$\frac{1}{2}$ lbs	ripe mangos, peeled, pitted and chopped	1.25 kg
$\frac{1}{2}$ cup	granulated sugar	125 mL
1 cup	whipping (35%) cream	250 mL

FROSTING

1 cup	whipping (35%) cream	250 mL
1 tbsp	confectioner's (icing) sugar	15 mL
2 tsp	orange liqueur	10 mL
1$\frac{1}{2}$ cups	toasted sliced almonds	375 mL
1	mango, peeled, pitted and sliced	1

1. **Cake:** In a large mixer bowl, combine cake mix, eggs, orange zest and juice and oil. Beat on medium speed for 2 minutes. Spread batter in prepared pans, dividing evenly. Bake for 30 to 35 minutes or until a tester inserted in the center comes out clean. Cool 10 minutes in pans on a wire rack, then remove from pans and cool completely on rack. Freeze 1 cake layer for later use. With a long, sharp knife, cut remaining cake horizontally in half.

2. *Mango Mousse:* In a small bowl, sprinkle gelatin over orange liqueur. Let soften for 10 minutes. Purée mangos in food processor until smooth. You should have $2\frac{1}{2}$ cups (625 mL). Set aside any extra for garnish. In a large bowl, stir sugar into purée. Warm gelatin mixture in microwave or over simmering water until dissolved. Stir into mango purée. In a large mixer bowl, beat cream to stiff peaks. Fold into mango purée, gently but thoroughly.

3. *Assembly:* Place bottom cake layer cut-side up in springform pan. Spread mango mousse on top. Place top cake layer cut-side down over mousse. Press down lightly. Cover with plastic wrap and chill 4 hours or overnight.

4. *Frosting:* In a large mixer bowl, beat cream, confectioner's sugar and liqueur to stiff peaks. Release pan sides. Transfer cake to serving plate. Frost top and sides of cake with cream mixture. Press almonds onto sides. Decorate top with mango slices. Brush slices lightly with any reserved mango purée. Refrigerate until serving. Store leftover dessert in the refrigerator.

Hot Fudge Pudding Cake

Preheat oven to 400°F (200°C)
13- by 9-inch (3 L) cake pan, greased

SERVES 12 TO 16

Cake and sauce together in one pan! Chocolate lovers will really enjoy this, especially with a dollop of whipped cream or ice cream.

Tip
To bring out their flavor, toast pecans on a baking sheet at 350°F (180°C) for 10 minutes, stirring occasionally.

Variation
For a more chocolatey taste, use a dark chocolate cake mix.

1	pkg (18.25 oz/515 g) devil's food cake mix	1
2	eggs	2
1 cup	water	250 mL
1 cup	chopped pecans	250 mL
¾ cup	packed brown sugar	175 mL
½ cup	granulated sugar	125 mL
¼ cup	unsweetened cocoa powder, sifted	50 mL
2½ cups	boiling water	625 mL

1. In a large mixer bowl, combine cake mix, eggs and water. Beat on medium speed for 2 minutes. Stir in pecans. Spread evenly in prepared pan.

2. In a small bowl, combine brown sugar, granulated sugar and cocoa. Sprinkle over batter. Pour boiling water gently over top. Do not stir. Bake for 40 to 45 minutes or until set. Serve warm.

Chewy Coconut Nut Bars *(page 146)* ▶

Apple Coconut Crumble

Preheat oven to 350°F (180°C)
13- by 9-inch (3 L) cake pan, greased

SERVES ABOUT 12

This simple dessert is always a favorite.

Tips
Keep apple slices quite chunky, especially when apples are older, to ensure that they don't become mushy in baking.

Freeze dollops of whipped cream for an easy garnish. Drop sweetened whipped cream in mounds onto waxed paper. Freeze uncovered until firm, about 2 hours. To use, simply lift onto your dessert and let thaw for 15 minutes.

Variation
Add 1 cup (250 mL) fresh or frozen cranberries to the apples.

1	pkg (18.25 oz/515 g) white or yellow cake mix	1
1 cup	flaked coconut	250 mL
1/2 cup	butter	125 mL
8	large apples, peeled, cored and cut in eighths (about 8 cups/2 L)	8
1 cup	water	250 mL
1/3 cup	lemon juice	75 mL
	Ice cream or whipped cream, optional	

1. In a large bowl, combine cake mix and coconut. Cut in butter with pastry blender or two knives until crumbly. Place apple slices in prepared pan. Sprinkle cake mixture over apples. Combine water and lemon juice. Pour evenly over crumble, moistening as much as possible. Bake for 45 to 55 minutes or until top is light golden and apples are tender. Serve warm or cool with ice cream or a dollop of whipped cream, if desired.

Lemon Berries 'n' Cream Cake

Preheat oven to 350°F (180°C)
Two 9-inch (23 cm) round cake pans, greased and floured

SERVES 12 TO 16

Here's a stunning summertime dessert that is perfect for special occasions.

Tips
Prepare lemon curd up to 1 week in advance. Double the recipe to have some on hand. It's nice as a filling for mini tart shells, garnished with fresh berries. It also makes a delicious topping for fresh fruit with whipped cream folded in.

Be careful not to boil lemon curd because it will curdle and thin out.

LEMON CURD FILLING

1	envelope (¼ oz/7 g or 1 tbsp/15 mL) unflavored gelatin	1
1 tbsp	water	15 mL
½ cup	granulated sugar	125 mL
2 tsp	grated lemon zest	10 mL
¼ cup	fresh lemon juice	50 mL
3	egg yolks	3
¼ cup	butter, diced	50 mL

CAKE

1	pkg (18.25 oz/515 g) white cake mix	1
1 tbsp	grated lemon zest	15 mL

FROSTING & FILLING

3 cups	whipping (35%) cream	750 mL
⅓ cup	confectioner's (icing) sugar, sifted	75 mL
3 cups	fresh strawberries	750 mL
1 cup	fresh blueberries	250 mL

1. **Lemon Curd:** In a small bowl, sprinkle gelatin over water. Let soften for 10 minutes. In a small saucepan, combine sugar, lemon zest and juice and egg yolks. Whisk to blend. Add butter. Cook over medium heat, stirring constantly until mixture thickens and leaves a path on back of spoon when finger is drawn across, about 7 minutes. Do not boil. Remove from heat. Add gelatin mixture. Stir to dissolve. Cover tightly with plastic wrap pressing against the surface to prevent a skin from forming. Chill thoroughly.

Variations
Replace blueberries with blackberries or raspberries. Although a combination of light and dark berries is most attractive looking, almost any mixture will taste great.

For an extra hit of lemon, use a lemon cake mix.

2. *Cake:* Add lemon zest to cake mix and prepare, bake and cool according to package directions. Freeze 1 cake for later use. With a long, sharp knife, cut remaining cake horizontally in half.

3. *Frosting & Filling:* In a large mixer bowl, beat cream and confectioner's sugar to stiff peaks. Slice 1¾ cups (425 mL) of the strawberries. Set aside.

4. *Assembly:* Place bottom cake layer cut-side up on serving plate. Spread ½ cup (125 mL) lemon curd on top, leaving a 1-inch (2.5 cm) border. Scatter sliced berries on top. Spread 1 cup (250 mL) of the cream over berries. Place top cake layer cut-side down on cream. Spread remaining cream over top and sides of cake. Pipe cream rosettes around top edge. Place ring of strawberries around edge and pile blueberries in center. Refrigerate until serving. Store leftover cake in the refrigerator.

Pineapple Coconut Dream Bars

Preheat oven to 350°F (180°C)
13- by 9-inch (3 L) cake pan, greased

CRUST

1	pkg (18.25 oz/515 g) white cake mix	1
½ cup	butter, melted	125 mL

TOPPING

2	cans (each 14 oz/398 mL) crushed pineapple, well-drained	2
2	eggs	2
1½ cups	granulated sugar	375 mL
⅓ cup	butter, melted	75 mL
1 tsp	vanilla	5 mL
2 cups	flaked coconut	500 mL

1. **Crust:** In a large bowl, combine cake mix and melted butter. Using a wooden spoon, mix until well blended. Press firmly into prepared pan. Bake for 12 to 15 minutes or until light golden. Cool 10 minutes.

2. **Topping:** Spread well-drained pineapple over crust. In a large mixer bowl, beat eggs and sugar until blended. Add melted butter and vanilla. Mix well. Stir in coconut. Spread over pineapple. Bake for 30 to 40 minutes or until set and golden. Cool completely in pan on a wire rack. Cut into bars.

Apricot Crunch

Preheat oven to 350°F (180°C)
9-inch (2.5 L) square baking dish, greased

SERVES ABOUT 8

Here's a great dessert that can easily be made with a few simple ingredients that you likely have on hand.

Tip
Melt butter in a clear liquid measuring cup in the microwave. The handle stays cool, making it easier to pour.

Variations
Replace 1 cup (250 mL) or the entire quantity of apricots with peaches or pears.

Fresh berries are a nice addition. Mix 1 cup (250 mL) into the apricots.

3	cans (each 14 oz/398 mL) apricot halves, drained	3
3 tbsp	packed brown sugar	45 mL
1	pkg (18.25 oz/515 g) white cake mix	1
1 cup	packed brown sugar	250 mL
2/3 cup	chopped nuts	150 mL
1/2 tsp	ground ginger	2 mL
1/2 cup	butter, melted	125 mL
	Sour cream, whipped cream or ice cream	

1. Arrange drained apricots in prepared pan. Sprinkle 3 tbsp (45 mL) brown sugar on top. In a large bowl, combine cake mix, 1 cup (250 mL) brown sugar, nuts, ginger and melted butter. Using a wooden spoon, mix until crumbly. Sprinkle crumble mixture evenly over apricots. Bake for 40 to 50 minutes or until topping is crisp and golden. Serve warm with sour cream, whipped cream or ice cream.

Strawberry Custard Dessert Cake

Preheat oven to 350°F (180°C)
9-inch (23 cm) springform pan, greased
Two 9-inch (23 cm) round cake pans, greased and floured

SERVES 12 TO 16

This dessert is a knockout in appearance as well as taste, a good choice to impress guests.

Tips

Custard thickened with flour in addition to egg yolks is more stable and stiffer than an exclusively egg-based version. This makes it better for cake filling.

Prepare parts well in advance for easy assembly later on.

For an easy filling, prepare a vanilla pudding-and-pie mix using 2½ cups (625 mL) milk rather than 3 cups (750 mL).

Use flat-ended tweezers to hull strawberries easily.

CRUST

1 cup	all-purpose flour	250 mL
2 tbsp	confectioner's (icing) sugar	25 mL
⅓ cup	butter	75 mL
⅓ cup	strawberry jam	75 mL

CAKE

1	pkg (18.25 oz/515 g) white cake mix	1

FILLING

3 cups	milk	750 mL
¾ cup	granulated sugar	175 mL
⅓ cup	all-purpose flour	75 mL
¼ tsp	salt	1 mL
3	egg yolks, beaten	3
2 tbsp	butter	25 mL
1 tsp	vanilla	5 mL

TOPPING

4 cups	fresh strawberries, washed hulled and halved	1 L
1 cup	granulated sugar	250 mL
3 tbsp	cornstarch	45 mL

1. **Crust:** In a bowl, combine flour, confectioner's sugar and butter, mixing with a wooden spoon until crumbly. Press firmly into springform pan. Bake for 18 to 25 minutes or until golden. Cool completely in pan on a wire rack. Reserve jam until cake is assembled.

166

Variation
A mixture of strawberries and raspberries or blueberries is nice.

2. **Cake:** Prepare cake according to package directions and bake in prepared cake pans. Cool 10 minutes in pans on a wire rack, then remove from pans and cool completely on rack. Reserve one layer for another dessert. Cut other layer in half horizontally.

3. **Filling:** In a saucepan, heat milk over medium heat until bubbles form around edge and it is steaming. (You can also do this in a microwave oven.) In another saucepan, combine sugar, flour and salt. Gradually add scalded milk. Cook, stirring constantly, over medium heat until thickened. Cover and cook for 2 minutes longer, stirring occasionally. Stir a small amount (ie., about $1/2$-cup/125 mL) of hot mixture into egg yolks, then add egg mixture to hot milk mixture. Cook for 1 minute longer, stirring constantly. Remove from heat. Add butter and vanilla stirring until melted. Cover surface with plastic wrap. Cool completely.

4. **Topping:** In a saucepan, mix 2 cups (500 mL) of strawberries with sugar and cornstarch. Heat on high, stirring constantly until mixture bubbles and forms a sauce. Immediately reduce heat to low and cook until berries are softened and sauce is thickened slightly. Stir in remaining berries. Chill thoroughly.

5. **Assembly:** Spread jam over crust. Place 1 cake layer over jam cut-side up. Spread filling on top. Cover with top cake layer, cut-side up. Spread topping over top of cake. Chill at least 2 hours or overnight before serving. To serve, remove sides of springform pan and place cake on a serving plate. Store leftover cake in the refrigerator.

Pineapple Delight

Preheat oven to 400°F (200°C)
13- by 9-inch (3 L) cake pan, greased

SERVES 12 TO 16

The top of this tasty dessert is very light, almost like a soufflé with a crisp crust underneath.

Tip
If you can't find crushed pineapple (or buy chunks by mistake!), you can process pieces in a food processor until they are coarsely chopped.

Variation
Replace lemon cake mix with white or pineapple.

CRUST

1	pkg (18.25 oz/515 g) lemon cake mix, divided	1
½ cup	butter, melted	125 mL

TOPPING

8 oz	cream cheese, softened	250 g
4	eggs	4
2 cups	milk	500 mL
1	can (19 oz/540 mL) crushed pineapple, well-drained	1

1. **Crust:** Reserve 1 cup (250 mL) of the cake mix for topping. In a large bowl, combine remaining cake mix and melted butter. Using a wooden spoon, mix until a soft dough forms. Press firmly in prepared pan.

2. **Topping:** In a large mixer bowl, beat cream cheese on medium speed until smooth. Add eggs, one at a time, beating lightly after each addition. Beat in reserved cake mix. Add milk gradually beating on low speed until smooth. Set aside.

3. Spread pineapple evenly over crust. Pour cream cheese mixture on top. Bake for 30 to 40 minutes or until set and golden. Cool completely in pan on a wire rack before cutting.

Frostings, Fillings & Glazes

Basic Frosting Yields

The following is a guideline to the approximate amount of frosting you'll need to cover various types of cake. This information should allow you to create different combinations of frostings and cakes, without the frustration of running out of frosting before you've finished the job. If in doubt, it's always better to have a bit too much frosting than too little. Someone will always be happy to lick the bowl!

CAKE SIZE	FROSTING
13- by 9-inch (3 L) cake, top only	1½ cups (375 mL)
13- by 9-inch (3 L) cake, top and sides	3 cups (750 mL)
2-layer (8-inch/20 cm) round cake	3 cups (750 mL)
2-layer (9-inch/23 cm) round cake	3½ cups (825 mL)
8- or 9-inch (20-23 cm) square cake, ... top and sides	2 to 2½ cups (500 to 625 mL)
3 or 4-layer (8- or 9-inch/20 or 23 cm) . . . . round cake	3 to 4 cups (750 mL to 1 L)
12 cupcakes	1 cup (250 mL)
Tube or Bundt cakes	3½ cups (825 mL)

CAKE SIZE	GLAZE
13- by 9-inch (3 L) cake	½ to 1 cup (125 to 250 mL)
Tube or Bundt cakes	1½ cups (375 mL)

TIP • For many of the recipes, I have recommended one or two frostings that I think complement the cake. My selections are entirely personal and you may have different preferences. Feel free to experiment and above all, have fun with your choices.

Quick Caramel Frosting

MAKES ABOUT 4 CUPS (1 L) FROSTING

ENOUGH TO FROST A 13- BY 9-INCH (3 L) CAKE OR A 9-INCH (23 CM) 2-LAYER CAKE

This smooth frosting is particularly delicious on chocolate, banana and spice cake.

¾ cup	butter	175 mL
1 cup	packed brown sugar	250 mL
⅓ cup	evaporated milk or light (10%) cream	75 mL
3 cups	confectioner's (icing) sugar, sifted	750 mL
1½ tsp	vanilla	7 mL

1. In a saucepan, over low heat, heat butter and brown sugar, stirring until smooth. Stir in evaporated milk. Cool slightly. Gradually add confectioner's sugar and vanilla, beating to a soft spreading consistency.

Basic Cream Cheese Frosting

**MAKES ABOUT
3 CUPS (750 mL)
FROSTING**

**ENOUGH TO FILL
AND FROST A 2-LAYER
8-INCH (20 CM)
ROUND CAKE**

*This frosting is a
favorite for carrot
cake, but don't
limit it to that.
It's very versatile.
I particularly like
it on spice cake
or chocolate cake.*

8 oz	cream cheese, softened	250 g
1/2 cup	butter, softened	125 mL
1 tsp	vanilla	5 mL
3 to	confectioner's (icing) sugar,	750 to
3 1/2 cups	sifted	825 mL

1. In a large mixer bowl, beat cream cheese, butter and vanilla on medium speed until fluffy. Gradually add confectioner's sugar, beating on medium speed until light and creamy. Add a little more confectioner's sugar, if necessary, to stiffen icing.

Variations
Orange: Omit vanilla. Add 1 tbsp (15 mL) grated orange zest and 2 tbsp (25 mL) orange juice to cheese mixture, alternating with confectioner's sugar.
Pecan: Fold 1 cup (250 mL) finely chopped pecans into frosting.
Pineapple: Omit vanilla. Increase confectioner's (icing) sugar to 4 cups (1 L). Fold in 1/3 cup (75 mL) well-drained crushed pineapple.
Peach: Omit vanilla. Replace pineapple above with 1/2 cup (125 mL) mashed and drained canned peaches.
Berry: Omit vanilla. Replace peaches above with 1/2 cup (125 mL) mashed and drained fresh raspberries or strawberries.

Lemon Butter Cream

**MAKES ABOUT
6 CUPS (1.5 L)
FROSTING**

**ENOUGH TO FILL
AND FROST A
4-LAYER CAKE**

*This icing is
worth every
calorie. It makes
a lot, but some
is bound to get
eaten before it
reaches the cake.*

1 1/2 cups	butter, softened	375 mL
3 cups	confectioner's (icing) sugar, sifted	750 mL
1 tbsp	lemon juice	15 mL
2 1/2 cups	prepared lemon pie filling	625 mL

1. In a large mixer bowl, beat butter until smooth. Gradually add half the confectioner's sugar. Beat in lemon juice and pie filling. Gradually add remaining confectioner's sugar, beating on medium speed until light and creamy. Chill, if necessary, to reach desired consistency.

Rocky Road Frosting

This frosting, which is almost like fudge, is an ideal way to finish kids' birthday cakes.

Tip
Spread frosting while warm. It hardens quickly on cooling.

2 oz	unsweetened chocolate, chopped	60 g
2 cups	miniature marshmallows, divided	500 mL
1/4 cup	butter	50 mL
1/4 cup	water	50 mL
2 cups	confectioner's (icing) sugar, sifted	500 mL
1 tsp	vanilla	5 mL
1/2 cup	chopped pecans, walnuts or peanuts	125 mL

1. In a saucepan, combine chocolate, 1 cup (250 mL) of the marshmallows, butter and water. Cook, stirring constantly over low heat until melted and smooth. Cool slightly. Transfer mixture to a large mixer bowl. Add confectioner's sugar and vanilla. Beat on medium speed, to a soft spreading consistency. Stir in remaining marshmallows and nuts. Quickly spread over cake.

Very Creamy Butter Frosting

This is an extra creamy, buttery variation of a standard butter frosting.

Tip
Double the recipe to fill and frost a layer cake.

1/2 cup	butter, softened	125 mL
1 3/4 cups	confectioner's (icing) sugar, sifted	425 mL
1 tbsp	light (10%) cream	15 mL
1 tsp	vanilla	5 mL

1. In a small mixer bowl, beat butter until creamy. Gradually add confectioner's sugar and cream alternately, beating until smooth and creamy. Add vanilla and beat on high speed until light and fluffy.

Variations
Lemon or Orange: Omit vanilla. Add 1 tbsp (15 mL) grated lemon or orange zest and 1 tbsp (15 mL) lemon or orange juice.
Chocolate: Beat 2 oz (60 g) unsweetened chocolate, melted and cooled into frosting.

Basic Butter Frosting

*A versatile
frosting that lends
itself to a variety
of flavors.*

Tip
Prepare an extra
batch of this frosting
to have handy for
a last minute cake.
Store it in the
refrigerator for up
to 1 month but
soften to room
temperature to use.

½ cup	butter, softened	125 mL
4 cups	(approx) confectioner's (icing) sugar, sifted, divided	1 L
⅓ cup	(approx) light (10%) cream or evaporated milk	75 mL
1 tsp	vanilla	5 mL

1. In a large mixer bowl, beat butter and half of confectioner's sugar until light and creamy. Add cream and vanilla. Gradually add remaining confectioner's sugar, beating until smooth. Add a little more cream if frosting is too stiff or a little more confectioner's sugar if too soft to make a soft spreading consistency.

Variations
Lemon or Orange: Omit vanilla; add 1 tbsp (15 mL) lemon or orange zest and 1 tbsp (15 mL) lemon or orange juice.
Coffee: Omit vanilla; blend 1 tbsp (15 mL) instant coffee powder into the butter.
Chocolate: Add 2 oz (60 g) unsweetened chocolate, melted and cooled to creamed butter.
Cocoa: Replace ½ cup (125 mL) of the confectioner's (icing) sugar with ½ cup (125 mL) unsweetened cocoa powder, sifted together with the confectioner's (icing) sugar.
Cherry: Decrease cream to ¼ cup (50 mL). Omit vanilla; add 1 tbsp (15 mL) marashino cherry juice and fold in ½ cup (125 mL) well-drained, chopped cherries.
Cinnamon: Omit vanilla; add ½ tsp (2 mL) ground cinnamon to creamed butter.
Berry: Omit cream and vanilla; add ½ cup (125 mL) finely chopped or crushed fresh raspberries or strawberries.

Cocoa Butter Cream Frosting

**MAKES ABOUT
3 CUPS (750 ML)
FROSTING**

**ENOUGH TO FROST
A 9-INCH (23 CM)
2-LAYER CAKE**

3 cups	confectioner's (icing) sugar	750 mL
¾ cup	unsweetened cocoa powder	175 mL
⅔ cup	butter, softened	150 mL
5 to 6 tbsp	light (10%) cream or milk	75 to 90 mL
1½ tsp	vanilla	7 mL

Tip
Sifting the sugar
and cocoa together
elminates lumps and
blends them evenly.

1. Sift corfectioner's sugar and cocoa together. Set aside. In a large mixer bowl, beat butter until smooth. Gradually add cocoa mixture and cream, alternately, beating until smooth and creamy. Add a little more cream if the frosting is too stiff or a little more confectioner's (icing) sugar if it is too soft. (Add enough cream to make a soft spreading consistency.) Beat in vanilla.

Light 'n' Creamy Chocolate Frosting

**MAKES ABOUT
3 CUPS (750 ML)
FROSTING**

**ENOUGH TO FROST
A 9-INCH (23 CM)
ROUND 2-LAYER CAKE**

½ cup	butter, softened	125 mL
2 oz	unsweetened chocolate, melted and cooled	60 g
½ cup	(approx) confectioner's (icing) sugar, sifted	125 mL
½ cup	(approx) light (10%) cream	125 mL

*This delicious
frosting has a
creamy milk
chocolate flavor
that looks
particularly
striking with a
drizzle of dark
chocolate on top.*

1. In a large mixer bowl, beat butter and chocolate until blended. Add confectioner's sugar and cream alternately, beating until smooth, then beat on medium speed for 1 minute, or until light and creamy. Add a little more confectioner's sugar if the frosting is too soft or additional cream if it is too stiff.

Chocolate Sour Cream Frosting

**MAKES ABOUT
2¹⁄₂ CUPS (625 ML)
FROSTING**

**ENOUGH FOR A
9-INCH (23 CM)
SQUARE CAKE**

This frosting has a light, creamy chocolate color that looks and tastes terrific on dark chocolate cake.

¹⁄₄ cup	butter	50 mL
3 oz	semi-sweet chocolate, melted and cooled	90 g
¹⁄₂ cup	sour cream	125 mL
3 cups	confectioner's (icing) sugar, sifted	750 mL
2 tbsp	warm water	25 mL
1 tsp	vanilla	5 mL

1. In a small saucepan, heat butter and chocolate over low heat, stirring constantly until melted and smooth. Cool slightly. Transfer mixture to a large mixer bowl. Stir in sour cream. Gradually add confectioner's sugar and warm water alternately, beating on low speed until mixture is smooth and creamy. Beat in vanilla. Chill slightly, if necessary, to reach a soft spreading consistency.

Cooked Creamy Butter Frosting

**MAKES ABOUT
3¹⁄₂ CUPS (825 ML)
FROSTING**

**ENOUGH TO FILL
AND FROST A
2-LAYER CAKE**

This old-fashioned frosting is one of my favorites and worth the extra cooking step.

Tip
There's no substitute for real butter and real vanilla.

1 cup	milk	250 mL
2 tbsp	all-purpose flour	25 mL
1 cup	butter, softened	250 mL
1 cup	granulated sugar	250 mL
1 tsp	vanilla	5 mL

1. In a small saucepan, whisk milk and flour until smooth. Cook over medium heat, stirring constantly until thickened. Remove from heat. Cover surface with plastic wrap. Cool thoroughly.

2. In a large mixer bowl, beat butter, sugar and vanilla until light and fluffy. Gradually add cooled milk mixture, beating until light and creamy.

Flavored Whipped Creams

**MAKES ABOUT
2 CUPS (500 ML)
WHIPPED CREAM**

**ENOUGH TO FILL
AND FROST A 9-INCH
(23 CM) 2-LAYER
CAKE**

*This is the basic,
slightly sweetened
whipped cream
from which you
can make many
different flavors.*

Tips
Chill bowl, beaters
and cream well
before beating.

Double recipe
as required.

BASIC CREAM

1 cup	whipping (35%) cream	250 mL
2 tbsp	confectioner's (icing) sugar, sifted	25 mL

FLAVOR VARIATIONS (CHOOSE ONE)

1 tsp	vanilla	5 mL
$\frac{1}{2}$ tsp	almond extract	2 mL
$\frac{1}{2}$ tsp	peppermint extract	2 mL
$\frac{1}{2}$ tsp	rum or brandy extract, or 1 tbsp (15 mL) rum or brandy	2 mL
$\frac{1}{2}$ tsp	maple extract	2 mL
$\frac{1}{2}$ tsp	ground cinnamon	2 mL
$\frac{1}{2}$ tsp	ground nutmeg	2 mL
$\frac{1}{2}$ tsp	ground ginger	2 mL
$1\frac{1}{2}$ tsp	grated lemon or orange zest	7 mL
$1\frac{1}{2}$ tsp	instant coffee powder	7 mL

1. In a small mixer bowl, beat cream, confectioner's sugar and your chosen flavoring until stiff peaks form.

Variation
Fold $\frac{1}{4}$ cup (50 mL) crushed nut brittle, grated chocolate, chopped nuts, fruit or toasted coconut into stiffly whipped cream.

Chocolate Whipped Cream Filling & Frosting

**MAKES ABOUT 4 CUPS
(1 L) FROSTING**

**ENOUGH TO FILL
AND FROST 9-INCH
(23 CM) 4-LAYER
CAKE**

Tip
Add crushed
chocolate toffee
bars, for a change.

2 cups	whipping (35%) cream	500 mL
$\frac{1}{2}$ cup	granulated sugar	125 mL
$\frac{1}{3}$ cup	unsweetened cocoa powder, sifted	75 mL
1 cup	crushed chocolate toffee bars (optional)	250 mL

1. In a small mixer bowl, combine cream, sugar and cocoa. Chill for 15 minutes, then beat mixture to stiff peaks. Fold in crushed chocolate bars, if using.

Chocolate Ganache

1 cup	whipping (35%) cream	250 mL
8 oz	semi-sweet chocolate, chopped	250 g
1 tbsp	liqueur (orange, coffee, raspberry, almond), optional	15 mL

1. In a small saucepan, bring cream to a boil over medium heat, stirring often. Place chocolate in a large bowl. Pour hot cream over chocolate, stirring until melted. Stir in liqueur, if using. Let stand at room temperature until desired consistency is reached.

Variation
Replace semi-sweet with bittersweet chocolate.

To Use
Glaze: Let ganache stand for about 30 minutes. Pour evenly over top of cake letting it drip down sides. Let stand until chocolate sets.
Frosting: Let ganache stand for 3 to 4 hours or until a soft spreading consistency is reached. Spread over cake. Let stand until chocolate sets.

Jiffy Snow Frosting

1 1/4 cups	corn syrup	300 mL
2	egg whites	2
1 tsp	vanilla	5 mL
1/4 tsp	food coloring, optional	1 mL

1. In a small saucepan, over medium heat bring syrup to a boil. In a small mixer bowl, beat egg whites to stiff but moist peaks. Gradually beat in hot syrup. Continue beating until very stiff and shiny, about 5 minutes. Beat in vanilla and coloring, if desired. Spread immediately on cooled cake.

Chocolate
Cream Cheese Frosting

**MAKES ABOUT
2½ CUPS (625 ML)
FROSTING**

**ENOUGH TO FROST
A BUNDT OR
TUBE CAKE**

6 oz	semi-sweet chocolate, chopped	175 g
¼ cup	water	50 mL
8 oz	cream cheese, softened	250 g
2 cups	confectioner's (icing) sugar, sifted	500 mL

1. In a small saucepan, combine chocolate and water. Heat over low heat (or microwave in a microwave-safe bowl on medium for 2 to 3 minutes) stirring until melted and smooth. In a large mixer bowl, beat cream cheese and chocolate mixture on low speed until blended. Gradually add confectioner's sugar, beating until smooth.

White Chocolate
Cream Cheese Frosting

**MAKES ABOUT
3 CUPS (750 ML)
FROSTING**

**ENOUGH TO FROST
A 9-INCH (23 CM)
2-LAYER CAKE**

This frosting is devine on chocolate cake.

Tips
Use very low heat for melting white chocolate. It burns more easily than semi-sweet.

6 oz	white chocolate, chopped	175 g
8 oz	cream cheese, softened	250 g
¼ cup	butter, softened	50 mL
3 cups	confectioner's (icing) sugar, sifted	750 mL

1. In a small saucepan, over low heat, heat white chocolate until smooth, stirring constantly. (Or microwave on medium for 2 to 3 minutes, until almost melted. Then stir until smooth.) Cool to room temperature. In a large mixer bowl, beat cream cheese and butter until blended. Beat in melted chocolate until blended. Gradually add confectioner's sugar, beating until smooth, then beat on medium speed for 1 minute until light and creamy.

Banana Butter Frosting

**MAKES ABOUT
3 CUPS (625 ML)
TOPPING**

**ENOUGH TO FILL AND
FROST AN 8-INCH
(20 CM) 2-LAYER
CAKE**

½ cup	butter, softened	125 mL
½ cup	mashed ripe banana (1 to 2 bananas)	125 mL
4 cups	confectioner's (icing) sugar, sifted, divided	1 L
1 tbsp	light (10%) cream	15 mL

1. In a large mixer bowl, beat butter, mashed banana and half of confectioner's sugar on medium speed until light. Add cream. Add remaining confectioner's sugar gradually, beating until smooth and creamy.

Very Peanut Buttery Frosting

**MAKES ABOUT
3½ CUPS (825 ML)
FROSTING**

**ENOUGH TO FILL
AND FROST A 9-INCH
(23 CM) 2-LAYER
CAKE**

1 cup	creamy peanut butter	250 mL
½ cup	butter, softened	125 mL
2 cups	confectioner's (icing) sugar, sifted	500 mL
¼ cup	milk	50 mL
1 tsp	vanilla	5 mL

This creamy frosting has a great peanut butter taste. It's nice on chocolate or peanut butter cake.

Tip
Add finely chopped peanuts to frosting or sprinkle coarsely chopped peanuts on top to decorate the cake.

1. In a large mixer bowl, beat peanut butter and butter on low speed until blended. Gradually add confectioner's sugar and milk alternately, mixing until thoroughly blended. Add vanilla. Beat on medium speed for 1 minute or until mixture is light and creamy.

Basic Glazes

Glazes, quick and easy to prepare, are a nice altnerative to frosting. They provide a simple finish in both taste and appearance. Often drizzled over Bundt and tube cakes, they harden on cooling.

VANILLA OR ALMOND

2 cups	confectioner's (icing) sugar, sifted	500 mL
1 tbsp	butter, softened	15 mL
1 tsp	vanilla or almond extract	5 mL
2 to 3 tbsp	hot water	25 to 45 mL

1. In a bowl, combine confectioner's sugar and butter. Add flavoring and enough liquid to make a smooth pourable consistency.

Variations
Coffee: Replace vanilla in Vanilla Glaze with 2 tsp (10 mL) instant coffee powder.
Orange, Lemon or Lime: Omit vanilla and water in Vanilla Glaze. Add 2 tsp (10 mL) grated orange, lemon or lime zest and 2 to 4 tbsp (25 to 50 mL) orange, lemon or lime juice.
Pineapple: Omit vanilla and water in Vanilla Glaze. Add 1 tsp (5 mL) grated orange zest and 2 to 4 tbsp (25 to 50 mL) pineapple juice.

Chocolate Glazes

There are many recipes for chocolate glaze. Each is a little different but all are simple to make. They are warm to spread or drizzle and firm up on cooling. Here are a few of my favorites.

BASIC CHOCOLATE GLAZE

1 oz	unsweetened chocolate, chopped	30 g
1 tbsp	butter	15 mL
1/4 cup	(approx) water	50 mL
2 cups	confectioner's (icing) sugar, sifted	500 mL

1. In a saucepan, melt chocolate, butter and water over low heat, stirring constantly until smooth. Remove from heat. Gradually add confectioner's sugar, stirring until smooth. Add a little more water if necessary to reach a pourable consistency. Pour warm glaze over top of cake, letting it drip down the sides.

BASIC CHOCOLATE CHIP GLAZE

1 cup	granulated sugar	250 mL
1/3 cup	butter	75 mL
1/3 cup	light (10%) cream	75 mL
1 cup	semi-sweet chocolate chips	250 mL
1/2 tsp	vanilla	2 mL

1. In a saucepan, combine sugar, butter and cream. Cook over medium heat, stirring constantly until mixture comes to a boil, then boil for 1 minute. Remove from heat. Add chocolate chips and vanilla, stirring until melted and smooth. Pour warm glaze over top of cake, letting it drip down the sides.

Variation
Replace vanilla with 1/4 tsp (1 mL) almond extract and garnish cake with sliced almonds.

CHOCOLATE PEANUT BUTTER GLAZE

4 oz	semi-sweet chocolate, chopped	125 g
2/3 cup	creamy peanut butter	150 mL

Tip
This glaze works well garnished with a sprinkling of chopped peanuts or crushed peanut brittle.

1. In a small saucepan, over low heat, heat chocolate and peanut butter, stirring constantly, until melted and smooth. Spread evenly over cake.

CHOCOLATE BRANDY GLAZE

4 oz	semi-sweet chocolate, chopped	125 g
1/4 cup	butter	50 mL
2 tbsp	whipping (35%) cream	25 mL
1 tbsp	brandy or almond liqueur	15 mL

1. In a small saucepan, heat chocolate and butter, over low heat, stirring constantly until melted and smooth. Remove from heat. Add cream and brandy. Mix well. Pour over top of cake, letting it drip down the sides.

Variation
Replace liqueur with 1 tsp (5 mL) brandy or almond extract.

Apricot Whipped Cream Filling

**MAKES ABOUT
4 CUPS (1 L) FILLING**

**ENOUGH TO FILL
AND FROST A 9-INCH
(23 CM) 4-LAYER
CAKE**

2 cups	whipping (35%) cream	500 mL
¼ cup	confectioner's (icing) sugar, sifted	50 mL
1	jar (7½ oz/213 mL) apricot baby food	1

1. In a large mixer bowl, beat whipping cream and confectioner's sugar to stiff peaks. Fold in apricot baby food, gently but thoroughly. Chill until using.

Decorator Frosting

**MAKES ABOUT
3½ CUPS (825 mL)
FROSTING**

**ENOUGH TO FILL
AND FROST A 9-INCH
(23 CM) 2-LAYER
CAKE.**

This is a good choice when a pure white frosting is desired. It's nice for piping as well as spreading.

Tip
Colorless vanilla is available at cake decorating supply stores. You can subsitute regular vanilla in this recipe, but the resulting color will be off-white.

1 cup	shortening	250 mL
2 tsp	colorless vanilla	10 mL
4½ cups	confectioner's (icing) sugar, sifted	1.125 L
¼ cup	light (10%) cream	50 mL

1. In a large mixer bowl, beat shortening and vanilla until light and creamy. Gradually add half the confectioner's sugar, beating well. Beat in half the cream. Gradually add remaining confectioner's sugar and cream, beating until smooth and creamy.

White Chocolate Whipped Cream Frosting

MAKES ABOUT 5 CUPS (1.25 L) FROSTING

ENOUGH TO FILL AND FROST A 9-INCH (23 CM) 4-LAYER CAKE

This is a nice choice for a white or chocolate cake with fresh berries. White chocolate curls make a nice garnish on the top.

3 cups	whipping (35%) cream, divided	750 mL
2 oz	white chocolate, chopped	60 g
1/3 cup	confectioner's (icing) sugar, sifted	75 mL
1 tsp	vanilla	5 mL

1. In a small saucepan, heat 1/2 cup (125 mL) of the whipping cream just to boiling. Remove from heat. Add chocolate, stirring until melted. Chill thoroughly, about 2 hours.

2. In a large mixer bowl, combine remaining cream, chilled chocolate cream mixture, confectioner's sugar and vanilla. Beat on medium speed until stiff peaks form, about 3 minutes.

Lemon Curd

MAKES ABOUT 1 2/3 CUPS (400 mL)

This tart, lemony filling is delicious when spread thinly between cake layers.

Tip
Tightly covered, lemon curd will keep for 1 month in the refrigerator. It is delicious on toast and hot biscuits, in tart fillings, meringues or simply by the spoonful.

3	eggs	3
1/2 cup	granulated sugar	125 mL
	Grated zest of 1 lemon	
1/2 cup	fresh lemon juice (2 lemons)	125 mL
6 tbsp	unsalted butter, diced	75 mL

1. In a small saucepan, whisk eggs, sugar and lemon zest until thoroughly blended. Add juice and butter. Cook over medium heat, whisking constantly until mixture thickens and leaves a path on the back of a wooden spoon when a finger is drawn across it. Do not boil. Pour through a strainer into a bowl. Cool to room temperature, whisking occasionally. Refrigerate, covered, until ready to use.

Variation
Replace half of the lemon juice and zest with lime or orange.

183

Chocolate 'n' Cream Frosting

**MAKES ABOUT
4 CUPS (1 L)
FROSTING**

**ENOUGH TO FROST
A 9-INCH (23 CM)
3-LAYER CAKE**

*This frosting is
rich, creamy and
chocolatey. It
is also very easy
to spread.*

Tips
Use unsalted
butter for frostings,
if possible.

1½ cups	unsalted butter, softened	375 mL
½ cup	whipping (35%) cream	125 mL
2 tsp	vanilla	10 mL
3 cups	confectioner's (icing) sugar, sifted	750 mL
6 oz	unsweetened chocolate, melted and cooled	175 g

1. In a large mixer bowl, beat butter until light and fluffy. Gradually beat in cream and vanilla. Add confectioner's sugar, 1 cup (250 mL) at a time, beating until smooth after each addition. Add melted chocolate, beating until smooth.

Variation
Mocha Fudge Frosting: Add 2 tbsp (25 mL) instant coffee, espresso powder or coffee liqueur.

Liqueur-Flavored Syrup

**MAKES ABOUT ¾ CUP
(175 mL) SYRUP**

*This makes a nice
addition to cakes
you are serving to
company. The
syrup, drizzled on
the cut surface
of the cake layers
adds moisture
and flavor.*

Tip
Prepare the syrup
up to a week ahead
and refrigerate until
you're ready to
serve it.

⅓ cup	water	75 mL
3 tbsp	granulated sugar	45 mL
3 tbsp	liqueur	45 mL

1. In a small saucepan, combine water and sugar. Bring to a boil over low heat, stirring until sugar dissolves. Remove from heat. Stir in liqueur. Cool completely. Cover and refrigerate until ready to use.

2. To use: Drizzle or brush 2 to 4 tbsp (25 to 50 mL) over cut surface of cake layers before adding filling or frosting.

Variation
Use your favorite liqueur such as brandy, Amaretto, kirsh or Grand Marnier to compliment the cake.

Crunchy Broiled Topping

¼ cup	butter	50 mL
¾ cup	brown sugar, packed	175 mL
¼ cup	light (10%) cream	50 mL
1 cup	flaked coconut	250 mL
1 cup	chopped pecans	250 mL

1. In a saucepan, melt butter. Stir in brown sugar, cream, coconut and pecans. Preheat broiler. Spread topping evenly over hot cake. Broil 6 inches (15 cm) below element for about 3 minutes or until golden brown. Cool cake completely in pan on a wire rack before cutting.

White Chocolate Buttercream

MAKES ABOUT 6 CUPS (1.5 L) FROSTING

ENOUGH TO FILL AND FROST A 9-INCH (23 CM) 4-LAYER CAKE

This frosting takes a little more time to make, but it is well worth the effort. It is not too sweet — just rich and creamy.

Tips
Add 1 tbsp (15 mL) of your favorite liqueur along with the vanilla, if desired.

Unsalted butter is preferable in buttercream frosting.

6	egg yolks	6
⅓ cup	granulated sugar	75 mL
2 tbsp	all-purpose flour	25 mL
1½ cups	light (10%) cream	375 mL
8 oz	white chocolate, chopped	250 g
2 tsp	vanilla	10 mL
1 cup	unsalted butter, softened	250 mL

1. In a medium bowl, whisk egg yolks, sugar and flour until smooth.

2. In a saucepan, heat cream just to a simmer. Gradually whisk into flour mixture. Return mixture to saucepan. Cook, over medium heat, stirring constantly, until mixture comes to a boil and is thickened and smooth. Remove from heat. Add white chocolate and vanilla, stirring until melted and smooth. Press plastic wrap onto surface to prevent a skin from forming. Cool to room temperature.

3. In a large mixer bowl, beat butter until light and fluffy. Beating at low speed, add pastry-cream mixture ¼ cup (50 mL) at a time, beating after each addition just until blended.

National Library of Canada Cataloguing in Publication

Snider, Jill, 1947–
  Cake mix magic 2: 125 more easy desserts… good as homemade / Jill Snider.

Includes index.
ISBN 0-7788-0058-X

1. Cake. 2. Food mixes.
I. Title. II. Title: Cake mix magic two.

TX763.S643 2002   641.8'653   C2002-901840-4

Index

Christmas cream cake,
124–25
coconut topping, 107
flavored, 176
frosting, 64
  coffee, 104
  white chocolate, 183
garnish, 161
lemon torte, 49
lime cream, 76–77
pumpkin 'n' cream cake, 130
raspberry cream, 58–59

topping, 46–47
White chocolate
  buttercream, 185
  chocolate cake, 32
  cranberry
    loaf, 94
    orange cake, 78
  frosting
    coffee, 46–47
    cream cheese, 178
    whipped cream, 183
White chocolate chips

banana coffee cake, 90
coconut rum cake, 69

Y

Yogurt, 11
  lemon poppy seed ring, 71

Z

Zucchini
  chocolate cake, 72
    with cranberries, 35